"This whole "creating experiences" has been the rage for years. With Business Charisma, your organization does it naturally."
Cassandra Anderson, CAE
Associate Vice President
New York Insurance Association

"I have read many Business Leadership and Motivational Books on taking your Company and Team to greater heights, but I cannot remember the topic of Business Charisma ever discussed. Charisma can definitely take an ordinary business to the heights of extraordinary. It is what makes others remember you."
John Metzger
President, Gerber Poultry

"The points Kordell makes in Business Charisma are priceless if you're serious about driving a very special company. Please send me copies for everyone in my organization."
Chuck Violand
President, Violand Management Associates

"In today's "click here for immediate gratification", technology can often drive a wedge between you and the customer. The principals outlined in this show the importance of sharing genuine passion for the Customers success. When this powerful connection is achieved, your Customer will fight for you to win the business."
Ken Ripich

D1414260

"You can wrestle in the mud with your competitors, or make yourself unreplaceable with business charisma."
Preston Hoopes
Vice President
Alex N. Sill Company

My customers often struggle to find ways to "add value" customer service so they stand out. The Charismatic Service skills of this material are exactly the sort of thing they need."
Catherine Hakala-Ausperk
Executive Director
Northeast Ohio Regional Library System

"Business Charisma is like finding the "happily-ever-after" for customers. This is a no fail strategy for customer growth and retention. It also becomes true elixir for change agent type of individuals."
Emily Lipovan
President, Sattler Companies

Business Charisma defines this subject in a way to make your business stand out from ordinary with unconventional thinking that leads to greatness. Come and get the "ah-ha" moments!"
Robin Hryckowian, PHR
Director of HR and Marketing
Western Reserve Restaurant Management, Inc.
(Wendy's Hamburger Franchises)

A special publication to the affects of empathic and exuberant leadership. Kordell empowers us to unfold our own innate gifts to contribute to the fabric of our communities. A must-read for both emerging and seasoned executives.
Penny Murphy, CAE
President & CEO
The Empire State Society of Association Executives, Inc.

"I was one of the people who thought charisma was something a person was born with – you either had it or you didn't. A skill you can learn? Who would have thought! After applying the tips in this book we are building better impressions than we thought possible."
Faith Sheaffer-Polen
Director, The Corporate University
Kent State University at Stark

Kordell has this inherent ability to engage people. It is no wonder that this encyclopedia of charisma reads so authentic. Everyone who reads this book will learn something that can make them more engaging, in business and personally.
Robert (Bob) Cannon
Product Innovation and Sales & Marketing Advisor

"Charisma is the key differentiator between an ordinary business and a great one. The good news is we all have the ability to increase our charisma. Read this book, follow the steps, and crush the competition."
Dr. Phil Kim
Author of Zebras & Ostriches

Reading about Business Charisma is watching a vivid dance of powerful cultures and people, leading you to your own (and business) state of charisma.
Doug Johnson
Common Sense University

Business Charisma

The Magnetism of Personality, Presence, and Customer Engagement

Kordell Norton

A TRUE FRIEND !

Kordell

Business Charisma: The Magnetism of Personality,
Presence, and Customer Engagement
By Kordell Norton

Unattributed quotations are by Kordell Norton
Cover by GianRufin, with adjustments by the author
Layout by author

ISBN – Paperback
978-0-9793045-7-6 (ISBN 13)
097930457 (ISBN 10)
Library of Congress Control Number: 2015910795

Reference: Sales, Sales Management, Marketing,
Leadership, Customer Service, Creativity

eScholars
eScholars Publishing
Division of eScholars LLC
1764 Calvert Drive
Cuyahoga Falls, OH 44223, United States of America

Table of Contents

Business Charisma

Dedicated to Dea, Wade, Preston, Mitch, Tom, Andrew, and David. There are times for something beyond friendship. Thanks for being there during the storm. May we enjoy the coming rainbows together.

Business Charisma

Introduction

There is a place in everyone's heart for a select group of people and organizations. They changed your life in significant ways. Theirs was a magic that inspired. They lifted you with their ability to coach, mentor, and educate. Their presence and personality is almost entertainment. If questioned, you would most likely say they were part of what is best in your life. They have charisma. In a hyper-connected world, it seems that everyone is desperately searching for connectedness. We are looking for inspiration, for someone who *gets* us and can transport us to a better place. We look for those magical others who can inspire, lead, educate, and become admired fellow travelers.

This book is about the skills that will give you additional presence and personality. For your business, it looks at charismatic organizations that connect with customers in such a way that a relationship is celebrated.

Based on research and surveys, it identifies organizations that the customer feels are not replaceable. They have taken the customer experience to the next level. Customers do not buy *from* them; they have a relationship *with* them. How powerful these words are: *from* and *with*. The *from business* struggles with price competition, morale, and commoditization. The *with* business is different, connecting in a deeper way. Its customers are engaged and are often described as rabid fanatics. What makes them that way? What makes these businesses so connected that customers refer to them as *my business*? They say things like, "I need to stop at *my* Starbucks on the way."

They, the fans, are passionate about "their" Harley-Davidson motorcycles, Trader Joe's, Disney vacation, and Apple Computer products. In a world of mass customization and with the best price found instantly on any smart phone, your competition just got tougher. Customers want an ardent and personal relationship. They are imploring for a connection that brings something greater. Transactions fade just like the "stuff" we acquire. On the other hand, experiences, memories, and *relationships* find special places in our lives with their transformation abilities. These relationships with business and people transform in emotional, spiritual, and almost religious ways.

Consider the customers of one business who do unnatural things because of this relationship. In pictures, they are grinning. Their smiles reflect fun and conquering. They are standing on the Great Wall of China, or in front of the Pyramids of Egypt, or atop Ayers Rock in the center of Australia, or in the Himalayas with Mount Everest behind them. Their photos all have the same ingredient: people are holding a bag from Stew Leonard's in Norwalk, Connecticut. Their pics eventually make it back to the store to reside on a Hall of Fame inside the doors of this fan-favorite grocery store.

Imagine your customers creating a user group with other customers. They gather and mount motorcycle steeds and ride off for the weekend with your logo splashed all over their clothes. How do you make one of the worst quality products on the market and have the best customer relationships in your realm? Charisma. How do you compete in a world where Customer Service has morphed into an imperative for Customer Experiences? What comes after the experiences that make word-of-mouth-buzz explode? Charisma.

Charisma for a business is a magical power that attracts customers like a moth to a flame. This connection is like the Pied Piper who seduces and recruits. Once under its influence, the customer brings others to share that magic. This special something vacuums up customers with its warmth and personality.

After decades of helping organizations create experiences in sales, customer service, and leadership, we asked the question: What comes after the customer experience?

The Baby Boomer generation, gazing at the approaching twilight years, has a focus on meaningful life connections. Those under forty likewise, with their Muppet like view, want connections with the *charismatic*!

Charisma is found in the medical practice of Dr. Shelby Cash of Hudson, Ohio. The warmth of his bedside manner is legendary to the point that his office staff tries to keep him from accepting new patients. Somehow, they get through only to discover a quality of care that creates more ranting fans.

Charisma in business is a Wendy's Hamburger franchise in Oakwood Village, Ohio, where the local octogenarians gather on Tuesdays and Thursdays. On this particular Thursday, the parking lot is completely full. One of their members is turning 102 years old. Once the food order is politely taken and delivered, you might find yourself in a packed dining room. I was offered cake along with everyone else in the dining room, many of whom were not guests of the festivities. In how many fast-food restaurants will you find a six-piece bluegrass band playing, its members (very good by the way) made up of members of the birthday party? This is a Wendy's! Isn't Wendy's one of those "plastic and cookie cutter" businesses? The wait staff is beaming as they stand in birthday pictures. The manager discloses that he regularly goes to the baseball games of the kids of his customers. Charm and personality ooze from this restaurant. Like most businesses, one location can have charisma while the sibling location a few miles away is so . . . plastic. "Can I have fries with that, maybe a "Hallelujah"?

The Blue Door Café in my hometown of Cuyahoga Falls, Ohio, is a charismatic business. On those select days when they are open, the parking lot is crammed. People wait in line to partake of the fresh and changing menu. In fact, there is not a sign for the business to be seen anywhere. Anywhere. You would only go there because others raved and gave you directions. "You will know it," they say. "Just look for the . . . blue door."

Such examples of business charisma are within driving distance of my home. They exist within minutes of you as well. These are examples of that special quality to attract with this "divine gift" (from the Greek *charisma*, its origins taken from the Greek *kharis*, meaning "grace, beauty, kindness"). Charisma in individuals is intriguing (allegedly possessed by one of Aphrodite's three attendants, Charis).

Charisma for your business is imperative. Other words phrases used to describe charisma are: evoking appeal, allure, fascination, captivation, enchantment, and magnetism. Such qualities for a business become the ultimate marketing tool, creating a sharpening stone for honed leadership, and bringing the intensity of gravity to suck in customers.

You do not have to be Apple, Disney, or the Ritz Carlton to have magnetic quality. Developing charisma in a business or a person is like the piano student or medical intern studying to be a professional in their field. Once they have learned the necessary skills, such professionals produce a quality that is magical.

As we journey into charisma, we will first look at business based on surveys and research of the author. Then in the last portion of the book, we will explore personal charisma. I invite you to turn up your own personal magnetism with attention to a few new behaviors and skills. While you are at it, make your business the envy of the competition. It is time to amp up your culture and your personality.

Kordell

Chapter 1

Magnetic Quality of Charisma

*"In a world of the fake, charisma is
the ultimate form of authenticity"*
KORDELL NORTON

He had been kneeling down to help a very young customer.
This Disney Store cast member (Disney has no "employees"
per se; workers are all "cast members") rose from his knees and
brought himself to his full six-foot height, his gaze brightening,
a smile erupting, and giving me a Pollyanna "Hi, how can I
help you?" His warmth washed over me like a Caribbean wave.
I thought it incredible how quickly he created "this is too good
to be true" feelings in me.

So, was the cast member charismatic because he worked at a
Disney Store? Did an automatic sprinkling of Disney fairy
dust explode all over him and then his customers? Many
people see Disney as charismatic with their fairy dust of
"making memories" at the happiest place on earth. Since it is
the customer who assigns charisma—this special sauce that
infects the heart—you might think the focus of this book is
customer service. To short-change charisma that way would
do you a disservice. When charisma is found in a business,
everyone benefits: the business, the employees, and, of course,
the customer.

Charismatic businesses can charge more for their goods.
Their market capitalization is higher, employee turnover lower,
and worker engagement higher. Marketing costs are lower
because of the word-of-mouth buzz that brings others to the
magic.

In a world of the average and mediocre, charisma is that bright light on the horizon whose clarion call seductively entices. Charisma is that secret ingredient that engages the customer to the max and crushes the competition. Charisma anoints the leader with magnetism that draws customers with allure and magic. It moves beyond customer "Wow!" and then goes even further.

Two businesses have access to the same market, the same raw goods, the same marketing opportunities; but one gets a different outcome. One business takes carbon and turns it into pencil lead while the other turns it into diamonds.

Same Stuff ... Different Outcome

- Both Playtex and Victoria's Secret have access to the same Spandex, but have different outcomes.
- Both Hewlett-Packard and Apple have access to the same computer chips but have different outcomes.
- Both McDonalds and Starbucks have access to the same coffee beans, but have different outcomes.

Charisma turns the everyday into something special. It shuns the mundane. The world pushes toward the average. Think of the popular Gatorade campaign of several decades past that touted "I wanna be like Mike" (Michael Jordan). Our world whispers of success if we wear the right clothes, read the best seller, attend the right school with the appropriate sheepskin, live in a certain neighborhood, and have 2.5 achieving children. The race is on to fit in, to make our parents proud, and to win the game of "look at me!" Now you just need to look, sound and smell like everyone else who arrived, or so it seems.

Nothing is as approved as mediocrity, the majority has established it, and it fixes its fangs on whatever gets beyond it either way.

(BLAISE PASCAL)

Habits turn on an autopilot, making the everyday doable. Habits get us through the day, accounting for as much as 40% the daily routine.[1] If you were deliberately doing the mind-numbing, then your attention would not swing to the saber tooth tiger in the bushes. Average is safe, or at least it was.

Except for the occasional Pearl Harbor, most ships are safe in the harbor. They stay safe if they do not go anywhere. Status quo is so much easier than the challenge of exploring virgin territory. Doing the same thing, however, is the epitome of crazy. That sameness affects how your customers perceive you.

Another problem with the status quo is that it makes things become transparent. After you drive past the new building year after year, it loses its novelty. Soon you do not even notice it. For you readers who drive a standard transmission, do you even think about it as you drive? Do you think about tying your shoes? No, you're on "Autopilot." By the same token, so are your customers who are on autopilot, driving past your business? Can you afford to be unseen?

In our world of hyperactive change, the last thing we need is invisibility. The fear of the unknown—that path descending into the darkened forest—has a different weight when the competition is getting more intense. Still, the religion of most management teams is about fitting in and keeping the wheels on the cart from squeaking. The *drive to average* continues to infect, making inspiring leadership scarcer. Often management fights to maintain the status quo. Leadership, on the other hand, flourishes with strategic change and achieving significance.

To stand out we must fight against mediocrity, the average, the status quo. Those best at being polar opposite of the mundane are charismatic organizations.

Take buying shoes. The Customer Service movement of shoe buying moved onto *Customer Experience* with a Nordstrom's purchase. Taking the Customer Experiences to a new level occurs with[2] Zappos. Why? Zappos takes the simple transaction of buying shoes and makes it so transparently easy that you want to buy again. How can you make a web based experience magical? Get out your wallet and warm up the laptop.

The Mr. Coffee transaction is now the smiling face of the Starbucks barista. The customer experience of buying groceries becomes a mini-vacation when shopping at Trader Joe's. In the frenetic press of massive change and the drowning avalanche of information, there is a point where we abandon analysis and logic.

> *Where is the life we have lost in living? Where is the wisdom we have lost in knowledge? Where is the knowledge we have lost in information?*

> *(T S Elliott)*

When overwhelmed with information, emotion occupies the judgment seat. Charisma quenches thirst in the desert of change. Warmth and personality are served with this inspiring elixir of charisma. Anything less and you become just another store in the shopping mall of life, with the same elevator music and a different carpet color.

Business charisma offers its cradling comfort of vision, inclusiveness, and insights for both customers and employees. It should be a focus for you like a Wayne Gretsky quote: "I skate where the puck is going, not where it has been."[3] If we want more than success, then the real enemy becomes the average. *Charisma in business is not average.* For individuals, leaders, and the whole organization, pursuing charisma becomes the imperative. Charisma is historically so connected with a special divine gift that Max Weber, the godfather of charisma as a science, described it for individuals:

> ". . . a certain quality of an individual personality by virtue of which he is set apart from ordinary men and treated as endowed with supernatural, superhuman, or at least specifically exceptional powers or qualities."[4]

Many scholars consider charisma as a divinely appointed gift, and so it follows that only certain special souls are touched with this ability to connect. For business, a more apt description of charisma is what makes you so engaged that the customer feels there is no substitute. It is the pinnacle destination for a business. This esoteric *je ne sais quoi* has customers and followers coming back repeatedly.

> **Business Charisma makes you so engaged that the customer feels there is no substitute.**

Organizations exist for only one purpose: to help people reach ends together that they couldn't achieve individually.

ROBERT H. WATERMAN

How an individual attains charisma has long remained a mystery. People often plead ignorance when asked how they got this special quality. Perhaps it was a learned skill acquired somewhere in their life journey. Likewise, organizations do not always know where they got it. They speak of the many years of effort before they became an overnight success. Like individuals, businesses are often unaware that others perceive them as charismatic.

Insofar as charisma is assigned by those it touches (i.e., customers, clients, followers, and even friends), identifying, and even replicating it has been difficult. For individuals, recent research has identified how you can get it personally. For a business, read on.

Recently, I renewed a connection with a business friend who works for a very visible high-tech company. His job has him looking at the latest and coolest trends in innovative technology. What did he want to talk about? The Big Green Egg, a robust barbeque grill. He described festivals where owners of the Big Green Egg gather for the weekend. Each owner shares recipes and creates new brotherhoods, like a gathering of rock star followers. I asked what it was about this pastime that made the Green Egg so enticing.

He quickly replied, "Oh, I personally think the Big Green Egg is very charismatic, but I am not sure what makes it that way."

For owners of the Big Green Egg this assigned magic spills into weekend cooking events. Faithful followers gather to share their common religion as a tribe.

In the coming pages, we will examine the common qualities and behaviors that make businesses charismatic. Must you have them all?

Is Harley-Davidson known for their vision? Probably not. Perhaps their vision is what happens with leather chaps or that testosterone-inducing exhaust sound comes from a motorcycle. Is Victoria's Secret known for their ability to capture the creativity of their employees? Not really.

From our surveys and research (See Appendix A.), we determined eight qualities that are associated with charisma. Some of the charismatic organizations exemplify all eight qualities, others just two or three. All can stand as examples. At this writing, Apple Computer is still milking the infectious charisma employed by the late Steve Jobs. Unless some new stories or their BHACs (Big, Hairy, and Audacious Concepts (See Chapter 5.) come out of Apple, they may lose some of their magic. While one person may see Apple, Disney, or Harley-Davidson as charismatic, others think a trip to a Disney theme park a waste of time and money. Most do not.

What are the Benefits of Business Charisma?
Divinely Conferred Power or Talent?

When the customer determines that a given business has *it*, then the magic draws others in. The customers give themselves to that entity. In modern jargon, they become a tribe. A religious commitment blossoms as communities are formed. The word cult comes to mind as the "cult-ture" is formed. Is there a divine influence? Why else would this enigma, this eclectic force come into our lives? Think of those screaming and fainting mobs that chased the Beatles in the '60s.

Attractiveness

The ability to draw, mesmerize, attract, and compel is probably charisma's greatest single benefit. *Consumer Reports* gave Harley-Davidson one of the worst quality rankings of all motorcycles in 2014. Yet, Harley-Davidson was ranked number one for customer loyalty. Subpar bikes with devoted followers. How does that happen?

When someone praises a business, the trust and "Aw, shucks" factor give creditability to break down suspicion. The cost savings in marketing and sales alone is worth any effort to make your business more charismatic. Engaged customers want to tell others about the magic.

These mesmerized customers become champions who recruit others like so many Pied Pipers. We are becoming less trustful of institutions and their motives, and so we discount advertising messages. One marketing expert told me that only 14% believe marketing hype while testimonials drive believability to 94%. Charisma squashes mistrust. A trusted message builds upon itself.

Think of the powerful marketing message of "Got milk?" At first, it was associated with a pile of Oreo cookies or a bunch of bananas. The mind jumped forward to asking "How could you possibly eat cookies without milk?" The next tactic for the California Milk Processor Board (who eventually opened their brilliant advertising to all dairy farmers nationwide) was to incorporate the creditability of an inventory of charismatic celebrities. Each advertising spokesperson sports a milk mustache signaling, "Yes, I do drink milk, and I recommend you do too." The power of the charismatic endorsement is not lost on cows in Nebraska.

Today we have methods to find charisma that come from the feedback of the engaged. Not only does word of mouth carry its weight, but also immediate feedback becomes available. These instantaneous tools have names like RottenTomatoes.com, UrbanSpoon.com, and even Twitter, Facebook, and Yelp. The names will change, but the list goes on. Twenty years ago, a dis-satisfied customer would tell 26 people about bad service. Today with one bad episode, one stick-in-the-mud manager or a poor product offering, the customer reaches out with negative feedback to tens of thousands with a simple click on a "Post" button.

When the nation learned that Tiger Woods could drive a golf ball but could not drive an Escalade, he lost a certain degree of charm—his charisma. One California University estimated a loss of 5 billion dollars in brand value for his advertising sponsors in the first week after his Brentwood, California shenanigans. His Escalade escapades put a dent in the charisma felt by his sponsors.

Cut through the Noise

Recently I counted the number of sizes, types, and capabilities of Tide detergent in a big box store. Which of the 40+ choices does the customer pick? In another stop at a local drugstore, I counted 138 shampoo brands. How do you stand out in such a market? If you even hint of being average, you are on the mental-comparison spreadsheet of the customer with price as the deciding factor. Organizations want sales training to counteract a buyer focused on pricing. Now that information is free and readily available, those factors that make us stand out are even more important.

How can you tell the charismatic companies apart from the others? They are the topic of conversation. They represent those products that people want, indeed cannot live without. In the crush of marketing messages today, those touching the heart move toward charisma.

All recipes can be duplicated. Even experiences can be copied and reproduced by others. Car manufacturers buy their competitors' vehicles and tear them apart down to individual components for weight and pricing analysis. This "research" (copying) is then turned into similar products that are "given away" with $0 down and 0% interest.

For those who lack charisma, the scientific study of what gets the customer's attention is intense. "If I just do what XYZ did, then I will get the same results." No, you will be a copycat, a non-original. You become another face in the crowd. You must mess with the status quo. Charisma is found at the edge. It is an outlier. It is Einstein, Columbus, Robert Noyce, and Steve Jobs. It is the lone voice in the wilderness and on the road less traveled. It is a yellow Dyson vacuum. It is the quirkiness of the Amish-grown chicken of Gerber Poultry.

Appeal to Emotion

People (employees, customers) are drawn to charisma like steel to a magnet. Why? Charisma offsets the uncertainty that seeps into our minds with countless choices. How do you deal with complexity? Like a compass that seeks north, we draw on the heart and its attraction to the power of charisma.

We like to think that we make decisions based on our impeccable good judgment, our ability to analyze. The number of shoes in your closet is a testament to the truth that emotion has a bigger impact. Maybe that new set of golf clubs will be just the magic to win. How many fishing poles, drills, or dried flower arrangements does one really need?

> "You call these baubles, well; it is with baubles that men are led. Do you think that you would be able to make men fight by reasoning? Never. That is good only for the scholar in his study. The soldier needs glory, distinctions, and rewards."[5]
>
> NAPOLEON

The customer needs glory, distinction, and reward. Charisma appeals to the possibilities and can make sane men put their lives at risk. Ponder the emotion of seeing your loved ones with their faces alive at a Disney theme park. Dwell on emotion of the French fry extravaganza found in a Five Guys brown bag. Think of the romantic excitement of giving her that robin-egg-blue bag with the special jewelry of that Tiffany moment. Glory? Distinction? Reward? Yes, it is just like the emotion of the boss who sincerely listens to you and breathes life into your ideas. Just like the leader who inspires, the business that can inspire and poke life into the emotions of the customer has a distinct advantage over average.

Likes Attract

What we appreciate we appropriate. The rich want to associate with the rich. The criminal plots with his fellow felon. Winners want to learn from other winners. In a charismatic leader, the follower assigns power and influence. In a charismatic business, the customer votes with dollars, and bring others to the altar in the process: "You have got to come and experience *this* with me." These rabid fans recruit. How many dedicated websites track and speculate on the unknown Apple products that may or may not even exist? The Big Green Egg cooking grill gives birth to food events. H.O.G. groups ride to other Harley-Davidson stores for the familial memory and a souvenir T-shirt to boot.

Cult-like

A criticism of charisma is that it creates a cult following because of its "likes attract" nature. The misguided charisma of a Hitler or a Jonestown Kool-Aid fest is typically cited. For those who are either for or against the Pink Ribbon movement for breast cancer, there is still the power of a movement. Cults, or the more trendy term of tribes, have commonality of interest. When the customer associates with the morals and ethics of any organization, a synergy springs to life.

When I conduct workshops, I ask participants to share what they find so intriguing about charismatic businesses. Within minutes, the energy level of the group jumps 10 notches. These share-a-thon conversations bring out cult-like behavior.

Laughter erupts and the noise level of the audience rises as individuals share their own views and experiences.

Perspective

Power and authority are two different things. You can have one and not the other. "Many are called, but few are chosen."[6] This message hints at given authority and the lack of influence to bring about success. Many are the wounds that come from rearward fire. You can assign authority, but power comes from people. Power is given, and if it is has been given by those above, then it must be earned to be kept. (See Chapter 4 on the subject of power.)

Significance

You have successfully completed hundreds of classes, with the information learned often wiped away along with and the names of your teachers. However, there front and center, are the names of three, or if you are lucky, maybe five teachers who really had an impact on you. These people changed your life. They altered your thinking and often your dreams and aspirations. They, like the charismatic business, take you on a trip in time. (See Chapter 7: Time Travel.) These special teachers moved you past success and appealed to significance. "You are good at this. You can become so much more."

When he decided to dedicate the proceeds of one of his books to a charity, Ken Dychtwald was told by the receiving executive that he was like others who had done something similar. Said the honcho to Ken, "You are at that age where significance is more important than success."

Benefits of Charisma:
- Better leadership: Leaders with charisma are almost twice as effective.
- Power and influence. (See Chapter 4: Gravitas.)

- **Service** at the next level. Because charisma lives in the present, where we "take time to smell the roses," it is essential for customer service. Get off the cell phone and pay attention to the individual in front of you.
- Entertainment: Are you an artist, skilled in acting, music, writing, or painting?
Experiencing charisma is watching an artist at work. It is mesmerizing. It is entertainment.
- Participation: Charisma is a participation sport. If volunteerism and retention are an issue for your organization, then it is easy to predict that charisma, with its engagement and enchantment are missing.
- Appetites: We live more deeply on vacation, during spiritual experiences, when sitting at the feet of the wizard. That award-winning chef with their inspiring restaurant brings out the best. Customers and employees are starving for something more substantial. Charisma is the spice.

Better Business Metrics

- A 5% investment in customer retention can yield anywhere from a 25% to a 100% improvement in profits.[7]
- Charismatic business have often as much as a 50% higher market share.[8]
- Charismatic organization command as much as a 40% higher prices than generic.[9]
- 70% of all organizations want to move past traditional transaction sales to higher value sales to customers with whom they have a closer relationship.[10]
- Charismatic Organizations "Charge as much as 50% more in price."[11]

- "Satisfied Customers" get a 13% discount off normal pricing, but "Engaged Customers" get a 23% premium over normal pricing. That is a 36% difference.[12]

Better People Metrics

In her book, *The Charisma Myth*,[13] Olivia Fox Cabane points to several benefits of charisma. These include:

- More productive workers
- More committed workers
- More personal sacrifice
- Perform at higher levels
- Better performance reviews
- Higher pay
- Hire better talent
- Lower turnover
- Lower hiring costs
- Lower business costs, lower malpractice costs

The Charisma Qualities

Our research revealed the qualities that were charismatic in businesses. In order to make them easier to understand, we have categorized and distilled down the qualities into the eight MAGNETIC groups.

M = Mission: developing personal customer relationships that go beyond transactions to engagements that elicit "Wow!"

A = Arena: setting the stage on the customer experience.

G = Gravitas: clout over command; how power trumps authority.

N = Narrative: the imperative for industrial-strength teachers.

E = Eclectic: the unconventional behavior and the creative world of mavericks, mavens, and misfits.

T = Time Travel: Every day is Monday for those who lack vision.

I = Individuals: Uniqueness meets abundance (being 1,000% better than the competition).

C = Charity: the end game . . . significance above success.

Does a charismatic business need all eight MAGNETIC qualities? No. The diversity in our surveys and what is considered charismatic by individuals is diverse. In fact, some of the business charisma organizations might only exhibit strengths in half of the qualities.

Can organizations lose their charisma?

Yes. Changes in leadership, technology, and even the economy can cause a business to lose their charisma. Will Apple Computer continue its magic with Steve Jobs gone? Disney has gone in and out of that magical state with their leadership, employees, and guests over the years.

Under the leadership of Herb Kelleher, Southwest Airlines oozed charisma. After Kelleher stepped down, the new leadership was more oriented toward "the numbers." Consequently, flight attendants were less enthusiastic about working at Southwest. On a Southwest flight I was told by one attendant, "We used to serve on committees to improve various parts of the airline. Lately these committees have now taken on a quality of 'what-is-in-it-for-me?' thinking. We don't feel like we are listened to as much . . . and some of the efforts to boost our passenger-centric culture are just window dressing by management."

So, how can you become charismatic? What qualities can you steal from others to make you and your businesses magnetic? How can your business get this *je ne sais quoi*?

Chapter 2

Mission

Developing Personal Customer Relationships that Elicit "Wow!"

A clear definition of the mission is the foundation for leadership.
PETER DRUCKER

At 36,000 feet, the Southwest Airlines flight attendant came on the intercom and apologized to someone named Sharon. I thought, *who the heck is Sharon?*

"Would everyone please lower your window shades," announces the flight attendant. The plane cabin darkens as she continues to give us instructions. "Now, would you all please reach up and turn on your flight attendant call-button. Don't worry about it. Every one of them in the plane will be lit."

The rest of the window shades descend as the call lights brightly ding, awakened into sparkling service.

"Now, again, I need to apologize to Sharon. Sharon, where are you sitting?" asks the attendant. Ten rows in front of me someone slowly raises their hand.

"Folks, I need to apologize to Sharon. I forgot to get her a birthday cake. Would you all please join me in singing Happy Birthday to Sharon?"

There, more than five miles high, 150 passengers, ensconced in an airplane cabin that looked like the inside view of a lighted Christmas tree, hammer out an enthusiastic Happy Birthday to a complete stranger.

For Sharon (and those who were part of the experience), this birthday experience reeks of charisma. Who was responsible for creating the relationship with the passenger? Was it the flight attendant or the airline who gives their employees the freedom to innovate?

Creating charisma in business is the ultimate mission. Your relationships with the customer should be moving to this engagement. Customers bring their purchasing dollars, as well as others who give their contribution, with titles like employee, board member, or even vendor. Life is relationships. Charisma is alive in the best relationships, and so it becomes the ultimate tool for customer service, leadership, marketing and sales. When the helm of the ship is the focus, sometimes the winds that a customer can create are taken for granted. Charisma understands this. Too much focus on presenting removes us from being present. Instead you want a relationship *that the customer* looks forward to with longing. This personal connection lifts both the customer and the business at the same time. It is symbiotic. It is present. This is the mission and goal. Management must get out of the way.

"I am sorry, but our policy states . . ." is never a good response for creating charisma. Zappos has rules on their return policy, stipulating that the customer has 365 days to return their purchase; the shoes must be in new condition, that is, not to have been worn.

The 365 days rule is the personality of Zappos. It is novel and fresh. It communicates a trust that you are not trying to rip them off. Brick by brick they build a monument to charisma, and this from a dot com.

There was a time in the '80s when I worked for a company that sold personal computers. The organization decided to shut down its 100+ retail stores to eliminate real estate expenses. The new strategy was to sell directly to corporate America. Employees were given skills to take customer problems and "turn lemons into lemonade" with customized solutions. Every single employee sought to "create value for the customer." The result? The company earned a spot on *Fortune Magazine*'s: "100 Fastest Growing Companies" three years in a row.

One of my customers was invited to sit on a panel at the National Sales Convention. In front of four hundred sales people and various executives, the questions poured out. One question in particular created sheer terror in my customer who happened to be the first on the panel to have to field questions: "Do you feel your sales people have done anything above and beyond the call of duty to take care of your needs?"

He hesitated, looked directly at me sitting in the front row, and said, "I don't know if I can answer that. You see, I wonder if your local team is not breaking a bunch of rules to make me happy."

The response of the audience in the room started as applause and built into a standing ovation. Four hundred sales people were pumping their fists the air. His answer was resonating charisma. It smelled right. It cleanly testified to a focus on service, a personal relationship, and getting a customer "Wow!"

Everyone sat back down, but the president was still standing. The moderator asked him if he had something to say. I thought, *Uh oh, I am toast now.* The president said, "I just know that *that* was the perfect answer. That is exactly what we want every customer to think and say."

A message went out. After the conference, sales took off on a terror. It lasted until a cultural change occurred that took the focus off the customer and unwittingly put it on hitting some internal measurements. For a short time it was Camelot - charisma showered fairy dust on all the stakeholders— customers, employees, management, vendors, stockholders, and the list goes on.

Leaders are people who focus attention on a vision.
WARREN BENNIS

Getting out of the way of those who can create such personal relationships is half of the job. The other half is to provide the weapons for champions to create charisma. So why focus on charisma and the deeper customer relationship? *Customers do not care as much about what you do as they care about who you are.* Consider the purchase of a car. For example, the customer picks Volvo for safety or BMW for engineering. These purchase decisions are made on what Volvo and BMW stand for, not necessarily for their cars. Were there other digital music players before the Apple iPod? Yes. Nevertheless, Apple was "cool." This Apple connection is almost a religion with their followers.

The importance of *who you are* is reflected in an HBO special on the craft of humor. The comedians in the program were Chris Rock, Jerry Seinfeld, Louis C.K., and Ricky Gervais. They asked the question of each other, "Do people come to hear your jokes, or do they come to hear you?" "They come to hear *you*," was the unanimous response given by the four comics.

This "who we are" is so profound that employees carry this culture wherever they go. On one trip to Dallas, I was three miles from the airport when my Enterprise rental car got a flat, and there was no spare, of course. The roadside assistance driver called to find out my location only to discover that he was at the wrong address, a couple of cities away. When he arrived late, of course, he loads the car and proceeds to lose his way on the back service roads at one of the largest airports in the world. Tick tock, tick tock. Missed flight maybe? When we finally get to the special lot for disabled rental vehicles, it had a line of twenty cars trying to get past the guard gate.

"Please don't get me stuck in this place. I have a flight to catch," I say to the driver.

I look across the lot to see a young woman in a yellow rain slicker. "Excuse me, but can you help me get to the airport?"

The young woman, Sondra Ross, takes charge. She can sense my urgency and grabs the nearest rental car and slides in, rain suit and all. She tells me that she might be breaking several company guidelines, but she drives me directly to my departure gate. What is so special about that? My rental car was with Enterprise, and Sondra works for National Car Rental.

Enterprise understands the importance of building charisma with the customer. They have adopted measuring devices (Net Promoter Score) to focus on improving relationships. People like Sondra Ross take action, break the rules, and go beyond customer service. As an employee of National Car Rental, a division of Enterprise, Sondra had been educated in building charismatic and caring customer relationships.

When you are about to miss your flight, you do not care about what they do. You care about who they are. Are they acting at a higher level of engagement than customer satisfaction? Now there are those who think Enterprise Rent-a-Car tries too hard, that they are sticky sweet. Business wants vocabulary like grit, sand, and moxie. Business people tend to shun touchy-feely words like relationship, charity, and love. The latter are very personal words.

If a business wants to stop playing small and getting small results, then the focus on becoming more "of whom you are" requires a business personality. Personality in business is culture. Those who are most prone to succeed will move past listening to the customer. They will hear, understand, and get the full picture.

In a 2009 edition of *60 Minutes,* Steve Kroft interviewed front man Chris Martin of the band Coldplay. Kroft asked why Coldplay connected so well with their fans. Martin had an interesting take on understanding the customer's world. While they are playing in large arenas, the lighting for Coldplay is so bright that it blinds the band's ability to see the audience. The band noticed that when they played a song that the fans did not seem to care for as much, there were more silhouettes of fans leaving the arena through the portals on their way to use the restrooms. By this barometer, the band could tell what kind of music they should write and play.

The imperative is to move beyond mere listening to observing what they do . . . to HUG the customer.

Hear what they are saying.
Understand their world
Get the full picture

Hear What They Are Saying.

Hear what they are communicating. What about the things they are *not* saying? How many times have you been in a public rest room where it was clean and neat, but on the floor by the exit door was a gathering of discarded paper towels? The customers had just washed their hands and were leaving. Others may not have done the same. Sharing a germ-laden door handle was not in the customer's wishes. Looking for a trashcan in which to drop the paper towel used to open the door, then not finding one by the door, they drop the towel on the floor. Message sent.

Hearing *past* the words is vital for connection. The customer notices. Yes, they notice: paper towels on the floor, umbrellas by the dozens by the door waiting for the surprise storm, and free mints for garlic breath at your Italian restaurant.

At one IKEA store I noticed bottles of baby food in the cafeteria shelves. Now that is listening to the needs of the couple who is bringing their little ones on their shopping safari.

How does business think past transactions? How do you move past the sales and service of some widget? The answer is thinking in terms of the total engagement. Disney knows that waiting in line is a transaction. It is as much a part of the customer experience as the ride. The education found in how Disney studies the wait-in-line is profound. Like most charismatic organizations, they have to deal with being too successful at times. They think before and after the ride. The mission is to develop a relationship to make the transaction transparent, even non-existent in the mind of the customer.

Charismatic business connects to get feedback. At the *Mohegan Sun* resort in Connecticut, departments have weekly contests that track "A" scores in customer relationships. Each department is very aware of where they stand in this hyperactively focused contest. To get the best scores, the individual employees have to go past customer "Wow!" They must develop relationships where the customer wants to tell others about the experience.

The Magic+ program at Disney has the customer wrapping a special electronic band around their wrist. These "bracelets" allow you to frequent a Disney restaurant in the Florida Epcot Center, where a scanner senses you and charges your account for the meal without even opening your wallet. These bracelets provide your kids with a safe locating device that doubles as their own pass to the park. Disney appreciates the need for thinking ahead for the customer. With your Disney Magic+, you can set up your lunch reservations in the morning and the system that tracks you. The system tracks where you go in the park, what rides you frequent, even how long you stop at a particular store to shop. When you arrive for lunch at your reserved time, your food is hot and delivered immediately. They find you by means of your Magic+ bracelet. Oh yeah, and for the kids there are special add-on buttons that can be attached to the bracelet with their favorite Disney character (for a fee, of course).

Businesses want the sales and service department to be the ears and eyes to the customer. Is this enough in a competitive world of connections? When is the last time your quality department, finance, or manufacturing folks made a sales call? What about focus groups? What do response cards in your delivered products say? Suggestion boxes? Customer bulletin boards where they can fill out a comment card immediately and post for the world to see?

There are out-of-touch-businesses that incentivize their servers to ask customers to fill out a comment card. Who is serving who? In the movie *What About Bob?,* dysfunctional Bob (Bill Murray) keeps pressing with "I want, I want, I need, I need" until Doctor Marvin finally gives in. Do you really want your customers to finally give in and pay you a compliment after your employees badger them to do so? Do you serve the customer, or is the customer being asked to serve your employees? Be careful on feedback. Something that is a good thing can go awry very quickly if it is not executed well.

Getting feedback from customers can take you to places you would not have even imagined. This is creativity. Consider the insights of one executive who got this type of feedback from his customers who were also his employees. In his book *Creativity Inc.*, Ed Catmull, President of Pixar and Disney Animation, relates how the company wanted to get feedback from their employees. In typical business fashion, they wanted to decrease the number of "man weeks" it took to make a movie, i.e., from 2200 to 1800. "How do we tap the brainpower of our people?" they asked. Their invention was a day when all employees were involved in a massive feedback and brainstorming process. Some employees went a step beyond the wishes of management. "Why 1800 man weeks? Why not 1200 man weeks? Yeah, why not?" Questions were asked, different directions taken. There is magic in hearing the customer (in this case the employee).[14]

Understand the Customer World.

When a mother buys Michelin tires, a Volvo, or Jiff peanut butter, what is she saying with her purchase dollars? Does she want more miles out of the tires? Perhaps she loves that Swedish car styling? Maybe she is just making PBJs. In these three examples, the products pander to the love of a mother. Husbands and jobs come and go, but the kids and pets are forever.

When you understand the customer, your offerings morph. They connect with the customer's need to move to a new place. You connect at an emotional level. It is easy to pitch your features and benefits, but to connect with the customer's heart moves you into rarified air.

At Google (not one of the top fifteen charisma companies but an honorable mention), they think of how they can move past the search engine. Google wants to create technology robots—servants, as it were—who could look at your information and then proactively provide you with information or a service that would initially surprise and then be irreplaceable. One of their robots might look in your Gmail to find a particular note referencing an airline flight for an upcoming trip. Their Google software-robot goes to the airline's website. There, it gets a status update and sends you a notification. Proactive and service-oriented. Understanding your world before even you did.

At Apple, Steve Jobs had this kind of focus on understanding. What did the device feel like when you held it? Should it have more rounded corners? How did the box open? Did you know that Apple designed the box so that the exact number of seconds went by before the lid separated from the bottom? One one-thousand, two one-thousand . . . the anticipation . . . three one-thousand. One Apple store associate shared that this separation of the box lid from the bottom was timed to the second. Like Goldilocks, it could not be too long and not too short. Really? Who pays attention to that sort of stuff? Do you make your packaging so that it intentionally piques the customer's anticipation?

Get the Full Picture.

I am a soap stealer. If I am paying hundreds of dollars for a hotel room, then I am going to take home those postage-stamp-sized soap for the apocalypse. There is a box on a shelf dedicated to my attempt to corner the travel soap market. At least there was. One day the edict came down: "No more soap. You either use those up or out they go." For a period I used the various soaps, each extracted from the beige paper packaging. Then I calculated how long it would take me to pay my penitence. I noticed that one soap was on a mission. Cruising past the soapbox, I stopped short. There in plain sight was a blatant example of "getting the full picture." In the center of the box were a couple of bars that stood out. Mostly it was because of the wrapping. As I contemplated this particular kleptomaniacal moment, my mind wandered back to the exact location where I "acquired" my treasure. It was then that the memories came flooding back.

The purveyor of that particular soap knew that I would steal it. In fact, they counted on it happening. That is my story and

I am sticking to it. Their package was designed so that every time I walked by that box of soaps I would see their unique soap and relive my customer experience.

Why? Their soap was in a jet-black wrapper, opposite in color to all the competitors. The hotel property? Disney. The wrapping was black, with a stylish Mickey Mouse seemingly calling, "Remember us? Remember how much fun you had? Come back. Come back." Is Disney really that in touch with the lives of their customers? Do they count on you absconding with the soap in order to engage you far beyond your visit to their theme park?

The charismatic business must have as their mission this kind of personal relationship with the customer. You must hug the customer. The business must think, act, and contribute to the lives of the clientele, that is, go beyond the daily transaction of business and wiggle into customers' lives. You want to play into customer behaviors, emotions, and dreams.

The Disney mission is found discreetly everywhere, including soft drink cups and parking tickets. It seems no place is out of bounds. With their mission focused on building memories, Disney opted out of "Wouldn't it be nice if we . . ." or "Maybe, we could . . ." Their transaction grows into something more significant, becoming part of your world. You transform and it becomes priceless.

If we look closer at the language of business-customer relationships, consider the discreet use of the prepositions *from* and *with*. The customer buys *from* a business but connects *with* a charismatic business. You buy your groceries *from* the local market, but you shop *with* Whole Foods because together you are influencing the whole world. You buy underwear *from* a discount store, but *with* Victoria's Secret you feel sexier. You buy T-shirts *from* Target, but *with* a Harley-Davidson T-shirt you look and feel tougher. We buy *from* in transactions. We transform *with* charismatic businesses:

- Harley-Davidson: It is not about sitting on a motorcycle. It is about the open road and freedom.
- Disney: It is not about riding an amusement park attraction. It is about a make-believe world that creates memories.
- Apple: It is not about owning a computer. It is about creativity and seamless innovation for your mind.
- Starbucks: Well, that one is about coffee. Or is it?

Confidentiality precludes me from sharing their name, but I have a client who has a simple mission statement: "We invest in our customer's success." Their customers build everything from bridges to nuclear submarines. Their view is to connect *with* their customers. "We invest in our customer's future" is their simple direction. This leads them to make strategic purchases of very specialized equipment for unique abilities. This in turn delivers customer specific solutions. Some of their multimillion dollar investments are highly secret. How risky is a big investment if you know the customer wants you to have a certain capacity? Customers love them because they do business *with* them. When all things are equal, their offerings are not. This charismatic relationship with customers spills over into their employee population.

Transformation is charismatic. When you buy a Harley-Davidson leather jacket, you plug into possibilities.

Charisma in a business will need cohorts. You will have fellow travelers with whom you must connect. What is your mission and the mission of your customer? Getting the full picture allows you to engage for more than just a mere transaction. When you have a mission to give extreme service to all the stakeholders, vendors, and employees associated with your venture, then a charismatic relationship can start.

Charisma brings engagement before the customer values it, the kind of service that is extreme or even severe (in a very good way). Service constantly exceeds expectations, generating results that have to be so intense that the customer says, "Wow, they thought so far ahead that they put the soap in black packaging. Who is *that* aware of planning for the next trip?"

On one winter morning, I arrived early for a flight. I looked out the windows to see the fallow plane sitting dark on the frozen tarmac. The crew arrives and gate agents assemble. Slowly the flight comes to life. When I finally board the plane even though it has sat cold all night, the cabin is too hot. Then the immediate discomfort fades as bags are stowed, seats taken. That's when I realized why the airplane was so hot. The airline was not heating the air; they were warming the surfaces, wanting you to *feel* that the airplane was warm and inviting by overheating the cabin. Go Southwest.

Tiffany knows that their signature turquoise bag sets high expectations when given to a loved one. To get a visual aid for my presentations, I stopped in a Tiffany store and asked for a bag so I could talk about the effect that Robin-egg-blue bags can have on customers.

"Sorry, but we have a policy that the only time you get one of our bags is when you buy something," said the sales person.

Surprised, I explained that I would be giving them awesome visibility. "Sorry, I can't do it."

As I was leaving, the salesperson brightened and asked if I

would like a Tiffany catalog. The eighty pages and full color binding had the most beautiful photography and page design imaginable. Even if they printed in quantity and shipped the catalog from less expensive offshore facilities, this book would cost ten to twenty times that of their signature blue bag.

That Tiffany knows all too well the value of their bag (never mind the jewels inside) shows a religious adherence to their mission. They move past the experience, driven by a mission to create a *je ne sais quoi*--an above-and-beyond for the customer's expectations. They think ahead and have an alternative offer for the customer who is "just looking."

Thinking in past, present and future for the customer is one key to building a charismatic relationship. This "getting a bigger picture" thinking might be better understood with a concept from Robert O. Brinkerhoff of Western Michigan University. Bob's research discovered that only 20% of the impact of training occurs during the actual teaching interaction. His research indicates that 40% of the training impact happens before, and 40% of the impact happens afterward. His is the message of homework or of movie trailers. What happens before or after the engagement? How many field trips to an Apple store have your people made . . . not to buy but to observe and learn? When is the last time your team studied the strategies and methods of Starbucks? Forget the coffee; focus on the barista. How might this 40>20>40 formula apply to your customer relationship?

I was a convention presenter at the mentioned *Mohegan Sun* resort in Uncasville, Connecticut. While exploring the massive hotel/convention center/casino, I was studying the property map at a kiosk in the shopping mall.

At my elbow a voice asks, "Is there something I can help you find? I find that map very hard to understand."

Startled, I turn to meet Joseph, a security supervisor. After a short conversation, he gives me a guided tour of the monster property, including the 10,000-seat sports arena, three casinos, and the Lost Guest desk. Lost Guests?

Joseph shares with me that the *Mohegan Sun* provided a few of these strategically placed desks for those who are lost. At the desk is a person to help those who are indeed lost. One of their tools is technology that allows one guest to track their significant other (provided the other has the *Mohegan Sun*'s "frequent flyer" card). Security finds the lost guest and asks them if they want to be found. Do not jinx a hot set of dice. Finding the lost person is a 20% proposition. Having the Lost Guest desk is a 40% pre-event value. Being considerate of the lost guest who does not want to be found is a 40% post-event focus.

With the increased competition in gambling, the *Mohegan Sun* knows that an over-the-top facility is not enough. The constant rolling programming of performing stars, the gambling, and the shopping is not enough. The *Mohegan Sun* knows that casino competitors have the same slot machines. What

competitors do not have is a Lost Guest desk with unique people who are acutely focused on the customer.

All charismatic organizations (and people) know this applies to them as well. In Lowe's Home Improvement centers across the country there is a quiet brainwashing ploy that capitalizes on the Pre>Present>Post nature of developing personal relationships.

On a Saturday morning, you will find an aisle in the local Lowe's Home Improvement store blocked with parents and children huddled over various tables and even sitting on the floor. Lowe's has created a morning program for families with build-it-yourself kits. Each kit has parts and assembly instructions. Toy airplanes, wooden cars, and cartoon monsters emerge. The "Build and Grow" program ensures those generations will feel at home when improving their homes.

There is also a second relationship built with the kits. On closer inspection you find the items constructed are airplanes that resemble characters in a soon-to-be-released Pixar movie, each complete with logo and detailing. When the Pixar's Monster University was screening, Lowe's had projects that reinforced the story line. The kid builds the item on Saturday and then expects to see the movie the next weekend. Is this a devious plot by Pixar for ticket sales, a Disney vacation, or a can of home improvement paint? Sneaky, very sneaky . . . or brilliant?

Business should have a mission of charismatic customer engagements that are long-term. Get the kids to tell their friends so their friends can recruit as well.

In his book *The Ultimate Question*,[15] Fred Reichheld asks the question, "What are you going to tell your friends about the interaction you had?" The expectation is that your interaction is going to be so powerful that the customer will have to share. The customer becomes an ambassador.

Most organizations ask the question, "Will you tell your friends and family about your experience?" In reality they are saying, "Oh please, oh please, oh please help us out. We think we have it right, but we could sure use your help. Please tell others how awesome we are." Charisma does not beg. When the focus is on a business instead of the customer, then the weaker "Will you tell . . ." question pokes out. With a charisma focus, the sincere and educated focus is on the customer's desires. The charismatic interest, their whole engagement, the pre-event – present – post-event (40>20>40) are so new and fresh that the customer walks away thinking, "I have got to share this with someone else!" They have to. It is too unique. It is connecting. The question "What are you going to tell others?" is relevant.

If your business is afraid to ask the tougher question, then perhaps your mission is nothing more than platitude. In fact, a mission statement that is for internal consumption is not a mission statement at all. It might be a monument to egos likely created in some retreat or offsite meeting.

Were customers involved in creating your mission statement? Were suppliers and vendors contributing to the mission statement? Advanced math requires an honesty about motives that is hard to find. Self-justification is a very infectious virus that incubates into mediocrity. To step out of the shadow of the average and move to extreme service is, and should be your mission. You need to hug the customer. It is the foundation on which all the other charisma elements are built. Such a mission of an ongoing relationship is the cornerstone of business charisma.

My brother owns a travel consulting practice that helps customers find the right cruise for their vacation desires. Their organization has a comprehensive knowledge of all the different cruise lines and their inventory of ships, allowing them to guide the customer to the best experience based on budget, time allowances, weather, and time of year. In one of our discussions about his business, he shared the fact that Disney can charge more for internal cabins on their cruise ships.

"You mean external cabins, that is, those with a view of the ocean?"

"No, the internal cabins," he answered.

"How can that be?"

"What Disney does is to put a screen on the wall of the internal cabin where a window would normally be. It looks like a window, but what you see is the same view as those in external cabins see. It looks like a portal, but it is really a video screen of what the external cabins see. Except . . ." He pauses to get my attention. ". . . during the day, the screen comes alive with Disney characters who swing by the window on Rapunzel's hair or interact (by arrangement) with the kids in the room."

What started out as a limiting factor for other cruise ships becomes a positive weapon for Disney to get people to request an inside room. If your mission were to entertain all of the customers, why not think about your subpar offerings and think of ways to make them more attractive if not the preferred product.

How can you appreciate something you don't see? Zappos, the shoe buying company does it intentionally. They operate on the premise that your purchase be unencumbered by processes. Buying the right style, color, size at a good price, all without a bunch of "footwork" is too simple. If the shoes arrive but do not meet the customer's expectation, the customer sends them back and gets the right ones. No charge. Oh, and don't forget the 365 days return period. It is all too easy.

What happens should you need to talk to someone in customer service at Zappos? Since most do not get that chance, you don't experience customer service. Why would you if you got what you wanted and it met your expectations? My sister called to share her customer service experience. She was on a short hold when the recorded Zappos message said, "While you are waiting, would like to hear the joke of the day? Press 1 if you would, and we will save your place in line." I had to call to check it out. The joke was corny, but you almost wanted to press the button to hear another. Of course, the joke tellers are regular employees.

This is much like Disney and waiting lines. It is a 40% pre-event moment. Since there are more customers than time, Disney is constantly tweaking the wait-in-line. The Magic Kingdom must really be magical to manage the line experience. Programs like Fast Pass, MyMagic+, and pagers that allow you sit comfortably and wait until it is your time to get on the ride are a given at Disney where the customer experience is constantly adjusted.

Sounds like the Sam Walton story. He was asking his managers how they could make the shopping experience better. How could Wal-Mart improve shopping for the customer as they entered the store? Likewise, what about the post-shopping experience? One of his managers said, "Sam, I think our stores are great. I don't know if you can make them better." As you may have guessed, the hapless fellow did not last much longer at Sam Walton's Wal-Mart. The moral of the story? Don't argue with Sam? No. The message was that there is always a way to fine-tune the customer relationship.

While I was writing this book, I noticed the space under the Starbucks bar where the patron's knees are harbored. For six bar stools there were four plugs. Starbucks knows that they are not just selling coffee. They are a second office, a meeting place for their patrons. Today's customer literally needs recharging. I know there are times when I go into Starbucks (though I have never had a cup of coffee in my life) just to buy hot chocolate. Could the Starbucks fix not be about coffee? Might it really be a need for a charging plug or Wi-Fi? The hot chocolate represents a small investment for 110 volts and an internet connection. Starbucks makes a lot more on that hot chocolate than the expense they incur providing the electricity and Wi-Fi.

Is your mission to help your customers do *their* business, or do you really think they come into your business because they want your coffee, your amusement ride, or their flight? Those leaders who see their business as an extension of their customer's lives and interests will connect with business charisma.

Starbucks asks you your name. This then goes on the cup in marker before creating the art that becomes your Joe. When they call you up for your order, it is by name. You do business *with* them. Shouldn't we all know our customers' names?

I had been involved in a massive effort by a large company to make all of their employees customer-focused. Senior management wanted to reward the effort by inviting those involved and their spouses to the Ritz Carlton at Laguna Nigel, California.

As we pull up to the portico, several valets surround the car and open the doors and latches on the trunk. While one valet extracts the suitcases, another extends his hand and confidently introduces himself by name. I respond by sharing my nom de plume in return.

"Welcome, Kordell Norton, to the Ritz Carlton," he says loudly. "We are glad that you are here. If you will step into our reception area, one of our associates will help you check in. Don't worry about your bags. We have them handled."

As we enter the lobby we are met by another Ritz Carlton employee who, calling me by name, escorts us to the front desk. Again I was greeted by name by someone I had never met before, as we went through the incidentals process. Shortly another appeared at my elbow, addressed me by name, and escorted the two of us to our room.

Though it was my first visit to this hotel, I felt like I was there for just another evening at home. How did these people know who I was, and how did they know my name? It took me three days to discover how they did it. When the first door attendant opened the car door and introduced himself, I responded with my name. He repeated it loudly, enough that the bellhop thirty feet away spun on his heels and went in to alert the rest of the hotel staff. "Kordell Norton is here. Kordell Norton is here." *How very Paul Revere of them*, I thought.

Who thinks about the exchanges with the customer like this? How much focus have you put on the customers arrival? What about before they arrive? Do you have your "black soap" ready?

Do your customers want their actual name on your product like a Starbucks cup or a Coke? Do people wear your corporate clothing as a statement of their membership in your tribe like Harley-Davidson, Victoria's Secret, or that set of mouse ears?

Do your customers go out of their way to recruit others, to bring them to your establishment? There is something beyond power when your customers want others to join in the cause. When your customers give you feedback *and you listen and respond,* that sets up the caring that is charismatic.

Even with all of that focus, there are building blocks, behaviors, and practices that will help make you and your business charismatic. These resources will help to make you more entertaining, better at execution, and more able to leverage all of your possible resources.

So, off to the field of battle, that arena where business charisma starts.

A Parting Shot.

Write down what they are saying. Once you have established a charismatic relationship you can talk a lot. For now, capture their thoughts. When the customer or employee is talking, you want them to know that you are listening. Nothing says that to a more extreme than taking notes.

In our sales training classes we tell participants, "Until the customer admits that they have a problem, you won't have a sale." As long as the salesperson is droning on about their new gizmo, the customer cannot express their needs, internal politics, and a host of other issues. To keep salespeople quiet we have them write down what the customer is saying in a simple and yet sophisticated form. The customers are liberated because they feel like someone is finally listening to them. The salesperson discovers new perspectives from the forced listening. They do not assume that they already know the answer.

Leaders: When your employees are talking, try to write it down. They will open up and share things that normally you would not get.

Consultants: Write it down. Eventually, you will forget unless you are still lucky enough to have some youthful photographic memory. The client will consider you brilliant for your wisdom in getting their wisdom.

Chapter 3

 **rena**

Setting the Stage on the Customer Experience

"All business is show business"
SCOTT MCKAIN

Atop the cork bulletin board are the following words posted in large, bold letters: "**BRAG BOARD**." There the diehard fans post their individual trophies. Dressed in camouflage with unshaven faces, the customers kneel behind their big game trophy or hold aloft their record-breaking fishing catch. The pictures spill beyond the edges of the bulletin board in the entryway of a Cabela's store. Often unnoticed, it is part of an elaborately staged event. It starts twenty feet earlier with a special mud-removing brush for boots mounted in the concrete near the shopping carts.

Cabela's is epic in setting the stage. The polished floors are mirror like. A large hearth at the front of the store frames a blazing wood fire, complete with comfortable leather chair seating. Spilling out in front of the shopper are racks of clothing with the distant Cabela's mountain. The mountain is two to three stories high and is covered in taxidermy specimens of elk, deer, antelope, bear, moose, and other assorted animals. Its mere presence signals to the customer, "OK, we get your hobbies and interests." From the side of the mountain tumbles a waterfall, cascading in a pond. Visible through the pond's Plexiglas wall you see the live freshwater fish.

The customers come, often with their children and grandchildren. Next to the restaurant is an electronic shooting gallery for families. Everywhere is displayed the gear and gadgets just begging to be snagged for the next outdoors adventure. There is a section of furniture, bedroom, and office furniture in the most stylish camouflage. Cabela's just begs to be explored. The Michigan store is often rated as the number one tourist destination in the state. Said one business charisma survey respondent: "I love to go shopping there, and I don't even hunt, fish or hike."

Just as the "M" is about the mission of personal relationship with the customer, the "A" is about setting the stage—your arena. Life-changing experiences and events occur on stages. There are many names for these stages: stadiums, operating theaters, courtrooms, retail stores, wedding chapels, and courtside. Weddings, graduations, and religious experiences provide the stages for experiences. These arenas rapidly alter our lives.

I remember reading an article on the executives of Starbucks and Home Depot titled *The Experience Economy* by Joe Pine and Jim Gilmore. They voiced a need to get back to the basics of staging a customer experience. Grind the coffee beans in the store so all the senses are engaged.

In Cleveland, prior to major stage productions of various Broadway shows, a local expert, Joe Garry, who has spent his life in the entertainment business, brings his background in music and theater for his insightful *Broadway Buzz* pre-event educational programs. He educates and entertains, often telling stories of his first-hand relationships with many of the greats in show business. When I asked him for a good book on creating

a stage production, he recommended Thomas Schumacher's
How Does the Show Go On? I wondered, *Who is Schumacher?*
He is, in fact, Disney's highly successful producer of their
stage plays, including *The Lion King.* Staging and the arena
are basics to creating the environment for charisma to blossom.
Research reflects how transforming experiences are more
valuable than the transaction of purchasing "stuff."

Professor Ryan Howell at San Francisco State University
studied those who purchased "stuff" (transactions) versus those
who purchased experiences (transformation). Those who
purchased stuff, cars, clothes, and electronics felt they were
making a great investment. Their purchase would allow them
to enjoy the new thing for a very long time. On the other hand,
the research points out that the shiny-new-thing is taken for
granted quickly, losing the joy of the purchase.

Howell's research went on to reflect how those who looked
back on a purchased experience realized that the memory and
the transformation provided a better value for the individual.[16]

> *Regard not your stuff; for the good of all the land of
> Egypt is yours.*
>
> GENESIS 45:20

Purchased "stuff" is the currency of transactions. Conversely,
charisma is in the *experience* that is on a stage or arena.
Charismatic business goes beyond having "workplace." The
magnetic business has buildings, equipment, showrooms,
parking lots, and rooftops. All are parts of the stage, and each
is fair game to be part of the experience.

When you think in terms of setting the stage for creating a
customer experience, then you will start thinking like the
producer of a stage play. I think of my speaking engagements.
A professional speaker arrives early to check the intricacies of

the stage. There are not only checks of the microphone, but also kitchen noise, lights, and even the water on the podium to make sure it is not ice cold because that affects the vocal cords and the timbre of the voice. You also do not want your "houseguests" to arrive at a messy or cluttered dwelling, so business must consider every aspect of the business stage. Always! Always!

Today the customer enters their hotel room and finds a cockroach in the tub. Before they even call the front desk, the smart phone takes a picture and posts it to the web. Your "stage" must be examined now more than ever. Each customer shares their customer experience with thousands of people with just the click of a mouse.

Nido Qubein, High Point University's charismatic president, is a magnetic person and understands the importance of focus on the arena. Shortly after his appointment as their new leader, he started fine-tuning the student experience. It started with the bathrooms. He knew that when freshmen visit, droves of parents come for a tour with their progeny. For many students, this means leaving home for the first time. Mothers are looking out for their little "Jimmy." What is the one thing she will check in the dorm rooms? The bathroom. Initially Nido focused on making the bathrooms sparkle and shine.

Students tend to congregate on stairways, so Nido had staircases widened where possible and fountains added here and there. Mirrors were installed on landings so students could see what is around the next flight of stairs. "A lesson on awareness," said Roger Clodfelter, the Vice President of the Office of Communications at Highpoint. One large tree was removed (with multiple smaller tree replacements) that concealed the library. Why hide the beautiful architecture? Foot-worn paths across lawns were paved in an unspoken testimonial of listening.

The university's endowment blossomed. According to

The Nido Qubein Effect

	2005	2014	Growth
Undergraduate Enrollment	1450	4300	197%
Fulltime Faculty	108	260	140%
Campus Size (acres)	92	380	313%
Square Footage	800,000	3 million	275%
Buildings on Campus	22	128	482%
Total Positions	430	1400	226%
Economic Impact	$160.3 million	$464.5 million	190%
Operating Budget	$38 million	$178 million	368%
Study Abroad Programs	5	41	720%

Clodfelter, university assets have grown from $75 million in 2005 to $579 million in 2014. The impact of charisma is plain to see and measurable. The comparisons of assets growth between before-Nido and after-Nido are staggering.

High Point University's website is a great example of looking at the total organization's presence as part of setting the stage. Like the simplicity of Zappos in creating an almost transparent experience, www.highpoint.edu becomes a study in priorities, ease of use, and a visual feast on the focus of the student.

A visit to IKEA revealed a trashcan next to the door in the restroom. In addition, the men's room sported a diaper-changing station in a message to modern fatherhood. For the technically perceptive, the restroom had both paper towels and the Dyson air-blade hand dryer (Dyson is another charismatic company identified in our surveys). IKEA, good at thinking about the customer, also has an emergency call button on the wall next to the commode. Who is *that* considerate of the customer?

I recently checked on the restrooms in a Cabela's store. Sure enough, there on the way was placed a sign that read "Shopping with your wife at Cabela's is like hunting with the game warden."

What about those perks of having assigned parking spaces? What message does that send to the actors (employees) and customers when they walk by your space? "I am so important that I have my own space." The imagined privileges of position and reserved parking are sending a message about your culture. Consider that your stage and parking spaces are part of it.

There could even be an argument against assigning parking spaces to the "Top Employee of the Month" right up front of the store. This does marvels for the top employee's morale, but it also communicates that the customer is #2 in importance in having to park farther away and walk by an often-empty space. Might that empty space also communicate that "I guess they don't have time to recognize their employees since the space is empty."

Ask all of your stakeholders to phone, drive in, purchase, and give feedback on your staged "production." When you call High Point University, you do not talk to a receptionist. You are asked if you would like to connect with their *concierge*. Really? Regular businesses have receptionists who answer phones and check-you-in. Charismatic businesses have the services of a concierge who are there to help you facilitate your life. At High Point University freshmen students participate with other dignitaries in groundbreaking events, literally getting down and dirty with Nido Qubein. That is connection.

There should be places where employees can make a mess. That should be hidden backstage, not "on stage." Employees smoking outside the front doors of Wal-Mart is *not* charismatic. Walt Disney was obsessed with the entire visual experience. The gondola ride above the Magic Kingdom, for instance, required rooftops to be clean and free of clutter. How many hotels pursue powerful customer relationships to get their guests into expensive rooms only for the guests to open windows that look out on pipes or acres of non-descript grey roofing?

The impact of studying the stage in all of its impact was not lost on Apple's products during the explosive Steve Jobs era. He understood the importance of the look. Perhaps you remember the hidden signatures embossed on the inside of the original Macintosh computer of its design team.

Consider the beautiful, blue-hued sandstone tiles found in Apple retail stores. Jobs went to great lengths to import from the Il Casone quarry in Italy. He wanted the same stone and look as the Cartier store in Paris or the Museum of Modern Art in New York. Since individual stones vary in color, great attention was made to put darker stones in the front of the store where exterior light makes them match the lighter stones in the back of the store. The charismatic organization gives serious, very serious, attention to the stage. It is a religion, part of the cult. When is the last time your leadership team studied stagecraft?

When do you stop fine-tuning your stage? Never. That is part of the message of charisma—to change the status quo. The customer will come back just to see what has changed. You become part of their life. That is your mission. We "catch up" on the things we love, like family, friends, and the latest ride at Disney.

When Disney's Animal Kingdom Park opened, the tweaking and fine-tuning began. The wild animals on the African Safari ride would place themselves in the shade and near watering holes. Disney had to change foliage or jackhammer out watering holes and move them so animals would congregate and lounge where the guests could see them. Is your environment designed for employees or for the customer? What kind of music is playing in the background? Does it appeal to your target customer set? When is the last time you had a "secret shopper" telephone to get through to you? Have you asked a trusted friend, who would be a stranger to your business, to play the part of the customer and manage your business stage to become a better production?

When the last of my six kids went off to college, we downsized into a smaller fixer-upper. My wife, the Supreme Commander, loves fixing up old homes. Our new cave dwelling required repeated trips to Home Depot and Lowe's for the appropriate materials. You could have bought their stock and benefited from us single-handedly driving its value up. So it seemed. At the local Lowe's you arrive to heavy-duty timber carts waiting down the middle of the lumber aisle. You do not have to search and find the resources; you just load timber and unload your wallet. Common sense, right? At the orange competitor down the street, the customer has to search for lumber carts. I watched as one customer was asked to move aside for an employee who had to drive their mopping machine right where the customer was standing. There was a semi-polite request for the shoppers to move their carcasses but without even a slight smile. The unspoken communication was about pecking order. They had a job to do, and the customer's job of buying lumber and paying their wages were hindering them from completing their assigned route. They now had a clean stage, but a personal customer relationship was obliterated.

Like the proverbial fish, culture stinks from the head down. Culture builds charisma. While one retail store might connect with customers, another can miss it. Is it the employees or their supervisor who is at fault? A good example of missing the opportunity to develop a personal customer relationship is  comparing Lowe's and Home Depot when a trip was made to sibling stores ten miles away. Lowe's was more interested in selling the washing machine warranty upgrades than they were in talking to the real decision-maker—my wife. They missed it. The focus was on the transaction. Two parking lots away we ran into the charismatic buzz saw of a Home Depot employee who, with the skill of Dr. Franz Mesmer himself, coaxed three times our budget from our wallets for a new washing machine. She focused on the decision-maker, and that was not me. That listening thing really does work. Yes, charisma, that magical characteristic, may exist in one store while down the street their rivaling store goes about building and maintaining the status quo. "Would you move your derriere so *I* can get *my* floors cleaned, please?" Like a Broadway play, every aspect of the customer/employee exchange is watched.

Several years ago, before being acquired, Cingular provided an example of using their website to connect with their customer (future employee). Those who wanted to work for this monolith had to navigate their website to find job opportunities. Screen after screen narrowed the journey until the would-be applicant finally got the heartwarming message, "Please paste your very cool résumé here." One phrase on a Cingular web page gave warmth and humanity to their stage.

The Land Grab of Charismatic Organizations

There is a reason that *arena* is a better description than stage for charismatic organizations. They believe in their cause, their vision, to the point where the resources of others are fair game for their own mission. This is similar to the Lowe's Build and Grow program. Disney hitchhikes on that program to extend their reach. All three benefit: Lowe's, Disney, and the customer. Is it marketing or is it strategy?

Consider Zappos. They have no permanent storefront, no public presence. Instead, they create it. On the day before Thanksgiving, they outfitted the baggage carousel at a large metropolitan airport with various prizes. Each slice of the carousel declared some prize. Haggard passengers gather to pick up bags and to participate in a *Wheel of Fortune* type game. If the customer's individual bag slides onto the appropriate "slice," they are rewarded by a Zappos representative with the correct oven mitt, cash, or other prize. Of course, since no one is going to see it—and you are Zappos after all—you make sure all the action goes onto that giant television station called YouTube.

As I type this, I am in one of my many offices. This particular space I call my "Starbucks office." With my hot chocolate beside me, I see customers coming and going, and they draw my attention. There is the girl with the fluorescent pink hair on her laptop a few tables away. Next to the fireplace are two wool suits, their brows furrowed in a deep conversation about the total domination of all humankind. Just my opinion. Although each square foot is merchandized, the core business of grinding beans and that permeating smell of their stage drifts in the air. The attention to detail and the environment for the customer is paramount.

Once I stopped at a McDonald's as an alternative to Starbucks for a writing location. Sometimes you do not have a choice. As I slid into my table, my knee banged against the sharp metallic corner of a square table leg. The searing pain made me take notice that Starbucks is not into knife edge metal legs.

In one Starbucks, I asked about Wi-Fi. The barista watched me attempt to log into the internet, but my attempt was in vain. She asked if I was successful, to which I answered, "It's OK, I will do something else with my time," I said. Then she asked if I would mind if she helped. Using her own password, she logged me into their network. Most organizations focus so much on the transaction (the 20% part of the exchange, the selling of products and services) that they do not even think that the customer might be there for another reason than buying their *stuff*.

When your organization only sees their job as producing widgets, then they have an internal focus. Charismatic businesses tune into what the customer is thinking. They have the smell of lifting up those served. They are thinking, *What can I do to my arena to make it a place to where the customer is drawn?*

Can you point to the power plugs in your business? Do those customers, be they plumbers, doctors, parents, patients, or even coffee drinkers feel comfortable at your establishment? If they sat for a few minutes, would they recognize that you have created a place for them as family members? Is your stage set so that customers can live their life *with* you? *Mi casa es su casa.*

Michael Vance, the former Dean of Disney University, shared the story of the fourteen-year-old boy who worked weekends as a "consultant." The boy would look at things and ask innocent and naïve questions that reflected insights and perspectives that Disney may have missed. Disney paid him $50,000 a year, and that was several decades ago! Disney was smart enough to know that the boy's insights were opportunities to fine-tune their offerings. If you were going to build a stage that caters to teenagers, wouldn't you need a fourteen-year-old consultant?

One of the boy's inventions was Five Sensing. We think in pictures. If I suggest "mother," for example, then my mental picture of auburn hair is probably different from your own mother. Disney's young expert offered the insight of "how can I make my customers [stage] experience better through the five senses of sight, smell, hearing, taste and touch?" In the production that is your business, with how many senses do you connect?

Movie theaters could cut their costs by buying popcorn in bulk bags. The smell of fresh made popcorn is purposeful in spite of the added cost. So is grinding coffee beans at Starbucks. A visit to the Hershey chocolate tour or Ghirardelli Square in San Francisco would be less impactful without the smell of cocoa.

What of sound? How about the sound the Starbucks espresso steam or Nordstrom's piano? It's a "Small World After All," as the song goes, with its incessant repetitiveness and mind-numbing torture lingering for hours. How can you take your negative customer experiences and turn them into your most demanded value? How can you appeal to the senses of your customers to make your business more charismatic?

The Art of Vacations

You walk into the store to see the employees wearing Hawaiian-themed shirts. You might see stuffed monkeys hanging from fake vines, ropes, and planks from sea-worn vessels. Over some of the shelves in one store there are thatched roofs.

You have walked into Trader Joe's, and you might forget that you are not on vacation. Trader Joe's knows that if you feel like you are on vacation, then you might feel more adventuresome. On vacations, you might try new foods or spend money on things you normally would not buy.

Trader Joe's makes their store a stage, a vacation theme platform. They make the shopping experience a pursuit of cool foods or life in a better place. The manager in one store told me that he sells two thousand cases of Three-Buck-Chuck (the affectionate name given to the Charles Shaw Winery bottles of vino) a week. The vino of a tropical beach bar is an easy mental jump for the shopper to make. Trader Joe's is a party just waiting to happen.

Trader Joe's hires crewmembers for their ability to interact with each other and the customer. *Strictly.* Bring the values and work ethic of Nebraska to the grocery store. Throw in a ship's bell and the fun starts.

One special aspect of Trader Joe's is their artist. One store manager told me that he had two full-time artists on staff. You carefully notice that the shelf signs all appear to be hand lettered. There is no computer generated look to mar the stage at Joe's. Consider the blackboard "canvases" with chalk and pastel artwork splashed appropriately throughout the store. An internet search of "Trader Joe's art" will reveal the creative license given to "copy that sells." Why wouldn't every business make signs that have a cult following?

Does your stage or arena warrant a cult, your own tribe? Are you trying to look like everyone else? Would your father be proud of your effort? Would he approve? Are you serving your father, or are you competing against Trader Joe's?

Your competition is Disney, Trader Joe's, and an Apple computer store. Those are some formidable foes. You are in the entertainment business, and serious work will move you to the next level as you consider your production and performances.

Magnetic organizations perform on a stage. Theirs is an arena where the audience is part of an event, or more accurately, an experience. A mediocre stage will not create exuberance of customers plodding, in lemming fashion, to the cash register. Without serious consideration of your arena, results will be predictable. Just look at your past performance. If you continue to do what you have always done, then all problems look like nails, and on . . . and on . . . and on . . ." drone the numbed masses.

Create the excitement of an arena. When someone starts using terms like "efficient use of capital," or "people, plants and property," carry those heretics off to the closest volcano. Beware the accountant or engineer who needs it perfect. Done is better than perfect. Hand-lettered signs are not perfect.

In my book, *Throwing Gas on the Fire*, I introduce the simple concept of "**DRASTIC**" for creating experiences. What happens when you consider life-changing events? What makes marriage, birth of a child, graduation, or a religious conversion so big in our lives? How could we change business to capitalize on the parts of a life-changing experience?

- **D**ollars - There are dollars involved, often in the form of admission fees. They might occur after the experience like souvenirs. At Disney, you pay to get into the parking lot, pay to get into the park, and you do not leave until you pay to have something with ears on it.

- **R**aiment - If you want to be in the game, you need to wear the uniform. This Old Testament term for clothing is seen in the wedding dress, the cap and gown, and even the doctor's smock. What clothing could you use to communicate, to enhance your arena? What is your wardrobe, your costume inventory?

- **A**uthority figure - Who is your expert, your who-said-of-the-greatest-magnitude? "By the power vested in me by the great State of _____, I now pronounce you man and wife." The Wizard of Oz had a magical power and authority. Isn't this magic given them by their followers?

- **S**ound - The wedding march, the Mormon Tabernacle Choir, the sound of popcorn popping at the movie theater. The orchestra pit can be replaced easily with the produced soundtrack . . . or can it?

- **T**hirst - Liquid is involved: beer at graduation, champagne at weddings, the baptismal font, the sacramental wine, the cruise ship.

- **I**llumination - Can you even have a romantic setting without candles? The massively produced rock concerts today ooze illumination with lasers and fireworks. How do you take a Ferris wheel and reflecting pool and make them special? Disney's Wonderful World of Color show must be experienced. How are you employing light in your business?

- **C**alories - The sacrament, the birthday cake, and chocolates from a loved one all speak to an experience.

Five Sensing

At Westin Hotels, they infuse a white tea scent everywhere. They want the aroma to be associated with the sumptuous hours you spend in one of their incredible beds. Every design artist is aware of the genius of the hourglass Coca-Cola bottle.

Both Chipotle and Five Guys have standardized chairs and tables that communicate both quality and cost consciousness at the same time with their "feel." The Chipotle chairs look like wood, but scrape one across the floor and the metal clang makes you think "tank."

How could you make your business arena better through the sense of smell, touch, tastes and so forth? What can you do to make your products not look and feel like everyone else?

Are you thinking, *This is just too much work?* Thinking of new ways to do what you do is work. Getting results is an expected outcome of charisma. It takes a certain chutzpah, an audacity. This boldness, nerve, and cheek all describe being magnetic. In addition, your job is to guide the ship. You must also leverage other resources.

A Parting Shot

It's all about the T-shirt. When people experience productions that are memorable, they want souvenirs. You can't leave Disneyland without something with ears on it. Those Harley-Davidson T-shirts "from far off lands" are trophies for those weekend road warriors in their cross-country sagas. Doesn't every father dream of returning from the big sports event with their child, pennant in hand and suitable for mounting on the bedroom wall? Graduating cap, the top layer of the wedding cake waiting quietly in the freezer for the one year anniversary, or tiny infant footprints in ink on a nursery wall. Souvenirs.

As a speaker, I know the better I connect with an audience, the more they want to keep the experience going. Book sales are higher. Do they want the book that says the same thing as the talk? Or do they want to keep the event going? Insightful management often orders a book for every participant. Drum home the message, or it stays as a reminder forever because no one ever throws away a book. Like the black soap, these things are reminders.

What is your T-shirt, your keepsake?

Chapter 4

Gravitas

Power Trumps Authority - Clout over Command

Superior work teams recognize that consistently high performance can be built not on rules but only on values.
DENNIS KINLAW

The key to successful leadership today is influence, not authority.
KENNETH BLANCHARD

When the crunch comes, people cling to those they know they can trust, those who are not detached but involved.
ADMIRAL JAMES STOCKDALE

Gravitas: high seriousness (as in a person's bearing or in the treatment of a subject); substance; weightiness. A five-ton canary can sleep anywhere it wants.

Charismatic organizations play to power. They understand that the ability to create takes substance. Authority is good, but real impact comes from power. The difference between authority and power is clearly found in the charismatic business.

Gravitas is the weight and influence that comes from power. Gravitas is the biggest gorilla in the room. It is the quiet confidence that authors build into the heroic character of an action film or paperback novel. Do not mess with John Wayne or John Rambo.

A classic example of gravitas is the management style of Jack Welch of General Electric. He stated, "GE be number 1 or 2 in each market segment, or else." Soon all employees had the pride of working for a company that only traded in winning. Gravitas does not ask for permission. It takes it. It is born of work, effort, and execution. The end game for gravitas is results. No matter the excuse, it does not change the performance.

Gravitas pays homage to authority, but it really respects and *worships* power. Therein lays a religious zealousness. The result is the tribe that bows at the altar of *culture*.

Since charisma is found in originality, which of the questions below foster innovation and freshness?

<u>Authority</u>
- How can I maintain the status quo (and my position)?
- What can I control?
- What can I do to others?
- What can be used up (what is my budget)?
- At whom can I thumb my nose?
- What perks can I get?
- Do ends sometimes occur with questionable means?

<u>Power</u>

- What things need to be changed (vision)?
- What can I make happen differently . . . better?
- What can I do to help others?
- What can I build?
- What self-sacrificing do I need to perform?

Bear in mind that pride (tearing others down) is anathema, and the moral thing to do is always the right thing to do. Gravitas as it relates to charisma is not what you can do *to* others but what we can do *for* others.

> *True leadership is the art of changing a group from what it is into what it ought to be. It is not something that is done to people; it is something done with people. By that definition, every person in your organization can and must lead.*
>
> VIRGINIA ALLAN

Power (Clout) versus Command
Which of the following paths do you take?

> **Authority** >
> Gives **Command** >
> Bestows **Management** >
> Maintains the **Status Quo** >
> Focuses on **Efficiency** >
> Pursues **the Known** >
> > "Yours is not to question why, yours is only to do or die"
> > Or, "To die for the company is to live forever."

> **Power >**
>> Bestows **Clout >**
>>> Empowers **Leadership >**
>>> Leads **Change >**
>>> Makes **Effective >**
>>> Pursues **the Unknown >**
>>> Realizes **Creativity** and
>>> Improvement>
>>> Gives birth to **Charisma.**

Many are managers, but fewer are those who manage *and* lead. Authority is the assigned responsibility to manage assets. Management will support the status quo to keep the wheels on the cart turning. They want no surprises, just performance using resources.

Power is a different thing altogether. Power and leadership maintain the illusion of calm and confidence while the duck is paddling like crazy out of view.

Substance comes from command *and* clout. The axiom, "Many are called but few are chosen,"[17] could well arouse the question, "You have position, but do you have power?" Does power come from position or from person?

True power reveals how we control ourselves. It is example. Its strength is found in "What can I do to/for myself?" It inspires, and draws like a magnet. It shines and persuades with the possible. Optimism and outcomes rolled up in one.

When change is the call of the day, we think the easier way is to have the power to push others—to use position to command. Although those who are controlled by this authority indeed execute, they often feel resentment. Respect flows naturally to power.

If charisma is the goal, then authority and the influence of clout should be the pursuit. Combine them both for wonderful outcomes. Is there anything quite as fascinating as someone who knows that they know?

Manager = Authority or Command
Leader = Power or Clout

The leader inspires, bringing customers back repeatedly. The leader knows that changing the status quo and taking all stakeholders to a higher place gets respect.

Execution is about tenure, morals, networking and the other parts of power. Such is the underpinnings to charisma.

The Same Ten People

I had a conversation with the head of a large and very successful volunteer organization. He was commiserating on lack of buy-in by the volunteers. A visiting leader from the "home office" commented to him that "It is the issue of STPs."

"STP?" asked the local leader.

The leader grinned and then said, "Yes, the Same Ten People. It seems that the same ten people are the ones who make all things happen in any organization."

STPs - The Same Ten People.

When companies build a culture that values gravitas, a foundational focus is on STPs.

A hallmark of STPs is their common denominator of power. Gravitas comes with power. Charisma is a downstream result of gravitas. Gravitas comes from those who make things happen, who drive down risk and relentlessly pursue results.

Authority is about command. Power is focus on clout and influence. You want both, but if you can only have one, it is better to have clout. Clout puts an invisible hand of influence on all outcomes.

In the book, *Power Base Selling: Secrets of an Ivy League Street Fighter,*[18] Jim Holden proposes a simple four-quadrant grid to understand power and authority. Although his book focuses on selling, the principle also applies to interactions

Authority Power	Authority No Power
No Authority Power	No Power No Authority

with others.

Power and Authority

Think Bill Clinton (a great charismatic). He had both authority and power. He was atop the food chain of authority as President, yet he had the power of the button of a nuclear arsenal—the ultimate power.

No Power but Some Authority

Think Al Gore. He could attend state funerals (authority) as Vice President, our stand-in authority figure. His real power came when he invented the internet. Not!

Power and No Authority

Think Hilary Clinton. She had no authority in the White House, well almost none by assignment. Did she have power? The nation was waiting to see the outcome of one of the most famous conversations ever had in the White House: "Bill, who is this Monica?"

No Power and No Authority

Think Socks, the White House cat.

Clout and power come from morals, action, networks, and contacts. You lose power by making bad choices and then justifying them. People with power know that mistakes are made. A mistake is an opportunity to learn and get back on track. Those who insist on justifying their bad behaviors lose power. Both a senior vice president who might have addiction issues and a Congressman who cannot hide his chorus girls lose influence. Although they may have temporary authority or command, they can eventually lose clout because of disregard for the conditions of power.

The mailroom clerk who is dating the daughter of the CEO has power percolating in his favor. This is the "Obvious Adams" who is pushed upward and forward. Those gaining power soon become the overnight success with their moral and ethical clout.

Are there markers that will guide you to those who have clout, influence, and power? Why do STPs seem to have it? Can you identify STPs in an organization? Yes, and here are their qualities:

- Moral/Ethical
- Tenured
- People oriented
- Networked
- Manage risk with added value
- Results oriented and able to make things happen
- They fall and get right back up again (practice, practice, practice)
- When change occurs, they are discovered.

Moral/Ethical

There is an ultimate judgment on those who are not ethical. As Ralph Waldo Emerson pointed out in his essay on compensation, we do not need to wait until some divine judgment bar in the heavens, for justice appears sooner than that. The immoral and unethical person has a "failure" gun pointed at them by others who see the injustice, the unearned gains, and feel a moral obligation to expose now.

Clout and lasting power come from the moral and the ethical. Warren Buffet (another charismatic) purchased American Express holdings in the 1960s. Meanwhile, Anthony "Tino" De Angelis, an executive who ran a large company that stored and distributed soybean oil, figured out that he could fill his industrial storage tanks with a top layer of soybean oil that floated above a massive water filled bottom. In doing so, he could defraud the bank with cheap water, and borrow larger sums of money. When his criminal antics were discovered, the banks who loaned the money went after the auditors of those tanks. They wanted the mess to fall on those who put dipsticks into the tanks and certified the inventory. The auditors were American Express. American Express contended that they were not liable. The price of American Express stock tanked.

Enter Warren Buffet. Recognizing the value (clout) that the American Express brand stood for, the young Buffet opened his checkbook to buy the unbelievably low priced stock. When American Express moved to take legal action to deflect the blame on De Angelis, Buffet stepped in. He counseled them to take the higher ground and take their lumps. The creditability of doing the moral thing resulted in a jump in the value of American Express stock. Buffet also did okay in the outcome as well. *Charisma comes from trust.* Trust is a byproduct of ethics and morality.

Tenured

Being unethical is always exposed in the bright noonday sun. Epic failures in judgment and behavior are shunned by the successful. The result is the issue of tenure. What of those who fail? If they get back up again and correct the flaw, trust is restored. When the unethical business tries to hide the activity by making excuses, the weight of judgment befalls them. The law of attraction goes to work. Likes attract, winners want to hang with winners, and criminals befriend criminals. Since charismatic organizations attract employees who have the values in the MAGNETIC, the unethical is thrown off.

The morals of STPs push on and last longer. STPs exemplify tenure, and though they lack title, the organization respects them with the highest regard.

People Oriented

Because they are ethical and tenured, the STPs evoke both respect and trust from others. People look to them for guidance and advice. At any meeting where someone has the assignment to communicate with a person that could not attend, most likely the absent one is an STP. Because STPs are people oriented, they carry a political power of likeability. Their combined warmth and presence is the personification of charity and service, which only adds to their influence. The strong get stronger so they can run farther, so they can jump higher, so they can become stronger, so they can . . . .

Networked

Jim Holden describes these owners of clout as "foxes." They quietly influence their environment. Wisely, they influence from the wings of the stage like Tonto to the Lone Ranger. "The whale that doesn't spout avoids the harpoon."

Since likes attract, foxes associate with other foxes. They have common interests in people, ethics, and making things happen. Their network of fellow STPs allows them to extend and even multiply their influence. Speaking on the subject of networking, Lee Iacocca (another charismatic) said, "Give me six of these guys and I could run the United States." If you find one STP and map their connections and conversations, you will find the other foxes. They talk, compare, and plot with each other. Often this planning and review is unofficial. It is done behind closed doors by STPs. If they could move forward in time, they would find that their conversations create turning points. All of this is without approval. Theirs is an agenda of success ensuring a compass course that will last. Might we say these STPs represent the Fox Network? Cheap humor, I know.

Managing Risk Downward by Increasing Value

The STPs may not have the skills or "know-how" to deal with the risks, but they can find someone who can. They know the value added by a vendor, makeup artist, or a great coach all bring additional capacity. Pride does not stand in the way of getting results. This is *not* the realm of the manager who foolishly touts "that is the way we have done it in the past, and that is the way we will always do it," as they move the life boats to a safe distance.

To move upward brings risks and the need for adding value or skills. A network brings value to the equation.

I watched them tear a building down;
A gang of men in a busy town.
With a mighty heave and a lusty yell,
They swung a boom and a side wall fell.

I said to the foreman, "Are these men skilled
As the men you'd hire if you had to build?"
He gave me a laugh and said, "No indeed!
Just a common laborer is all I need.
And I can wreck in a day or two
What it took the builder a year to do."

And I thought to myself as I went my way,
'Just which of these roles have I tried to play?'

Am I a builder who works with care
Measuring life by the rule and square,
Or am I a wrecker as I walk the town
Content with the labor of tearing down?"

(Anonymous)

Results Oriented

If it is counterproductive, why do it? Is being *efficient* the siren song, or should being *effective* be the focus? The STPs know that hacking at the leaves is a waste of time (an immoral pursuit) if the ladder is leaning against the wrong tree. If the mission will not support the goal, why even embark on the journey? The STPs ask one of the hardest questions, "What do we need to stop doing to move to the next level?" There is no sacredness in efficiently doing the wrong activity if it does not get results. Einstein said, "Insanity: doing the same thing over and over again and expecting different results." The results depend on the ethics, people, network, the tenure, and wisdom of fellow travelers and, of course, hard work. Such resources and qualities comprise the armor of the STPs.

If the road will not get you there, why take it? Is it about the journey, or is it the pursuit of the summit? Yes. The STP values the Sherpa team member because only then will they taste the sweet victory of reaching the summit. STPs value the journey and the pursuit of climbing the summit. Work we must, but do not forget to smell the flowers along the way.

Falling Down and Getting Back Up . . . a Story of Farms, Flutes and Football

Mistakes are something that people make. However, the mistake is not the person. It is something they did. STPs separate the two. It is falling down and getting back up. Mistakes cause reflection and evoke practice. Sports participation brings wins and losses. After each trophy or lack thereof come examination, practice, and improvement to win next time. Every music student hits wrong notes. The concert pianist was not born with the skill.

Doctors practice, as do lawyers. Seth Godin's fanciful rule of 10,000 hours to be a success is grounded in this doctrine. Do, evaluate, correct, and do again. Rinse and repeat. When Disney first opened retail stores in shopping malls in 1987, Michael Eisner, Disney's CEO, made a telephone call to their Human Resources Department. Eisner and Frank Wells (COO) had visited one of their new stores.

"Frank and I aren't pleased with what we have seen these past few days at the Disney Store," Eisner told them. "We noticed that the guest service experience isn't at the levels expected of Disney. The cast is not as friendly or engaging as they should be. There isn't anything differentiating the Disney Store from all the other stores in the Galleria."[19]

That call resulted in an all-hands-on-deck effort at Disney University. It was not that the people in the stores were bad. They were doing the same things as other mall stores, but Disney is not just another store. They are Disney. They create memories. The initial performance was evaluated and then a correction was determined. Cast members raised the level of performance with learned new skills.

That Disney Store performance is a stage play. Staged plays need rehearsals. Players need to practice. That is how Disney sees their world. As if an audience member invited to "come on stage," so Disney sees their guests entering the store. The Disney heritage moves beyond customer satisfaction. Other stores in the mall had customers, so Disney had to create something higher. Their cast members had to create a staged performance for guests. Store clerks sell, Disney engages. Perform, fail, evaluate, practice, and perform. Rinse and repeat . . . again!

In a charismatic business, the problem becomes the opportunity. Why waste time and effort on excuses, or reiterating policy? Turning lemons into lemonade distances the charismatic from the competition. The STPs personify this ability. As Nelson Rockefeller once pointed out, "Wherever we look upon this earth, the opportunities take shape within the problems."

How Do You Find these STPs?

Before change occurs, there is consultation with the STPs. Why? They are tenured. Theirs is a discernment of the endeavor. Will it work based on history? They command resources and know where the skeletons are. They network. STPs have the humility to admit what they know and what they do not know. The smart money is on the leader who wisely holds making a decision until they can run it past their influential and trustworthy STPs.

Charisma for a business mandates we embrace the STP qualities. We all need that grit, that sand of relentless pursuit. Fail, fall down, make the mistake. Develop the rare gravitas of getting back up. Courage is inspiring. Gravitas is inspiring. Does that make courage and gravitas interchangeable? Challenges overcome just beg others to study and learn. Why reinvent the wheel?

Entertainment is watching the great fall or the lowly rise to conquer. Entertainment then is the story. Gravitas in action creates the narrative of the story. Charisma is in the story narrative.

A Parting Shot

Overlooking the obvious is a common error. Gordon B. Hinckley called them "pickle suckers," that is, those cancerous members of your environment who carp and complain. They gather to suck the juice off the pickles and then quietly drop them back into the barrel. You can see them congregating, sharing common distain for the cause. On the other hand, the STPs—the Samurai warriors of getting things done—also congregate. Their calendars are full with many opportunities. They are not the talk of the proverbial water cooler because that is where the pickle suckers are discussed. They are in the middle of conversations.

Look at the obvious. Everyone else is. Once you see it, what are you going to do about it? If you do a stack rank of the troops, the lowest person represents the lowest level of incompetence that you will sanction. Do you really want to be that leader? The charismatic raises that level or carves it off. The charismatic also endows the STPs with resources and attention. What is the obvious? If you are not sure, then go to the STPs and ask. To them it is obvious all of the time.

Chapter 5

N arrative

The Imperative for Industrial Strength Teachers

*"The first principle was "Story Is King," by which we meant
that we would let nothing—not the technology, not the
merchandising possibilities—get in the way of our story."*
ED CATMULL
President, Pixar & Disney Animation

Salacious. The chain of lingerie stores had branding that
appealed to the male species in northern California. Customers
might buy *from* them, but they were not making a day-to-day
life *with* them. Not with the true customer, namely women. In
1982 women's underwear was sold in secluded sections of
stores where shopping for bras was something that was dreaded.
That all changed when the fashion expert arrived. He infused
them with dignity as well as style. Leslie Wexner, the founder
of The Limited, Bath & Body Works, and Express, worked his
magic and made the products feminine to a fault. The result is
Victoria's Secret, one of the top fifteen charismatic businesses
in our surveys.

Victoria's Secret is a great story. So are James Dyson's vacuum cleaners. His inventions were rejected repeatedly. So is the less than catchy name of Mortimer Mouse before it was changed to Mickey at the insistence of Roy Disney. What of the story of two Steve's, (Steve Jobs, and Steve Wozniak), displaying their history changing wares at the Homebrew Computer Club?

Narratives are the lifeblood of business. For the customer to share their relationship with your charismatic offerings, stories are an important tool. They help customers share their experience with others. "You gotta go there. They make the best what's-it sauce on either side of the tracks."

I was personally involved in one of these business stories. I needed it. It was a time when outcomes were not negotiable. No "maybe's" or "It would be nice to have."

On the evening of my thirty-fifth anniversary, my wife and I sat in a bright examination room to hear the somber news: "Kordell, you have cancer." The subsequent battle made me aware that many soldiers are included in this skirmish. I wanted the radiology people focused, the lab experts on top of their analysis. Even while I was under anesthesia, there were people unknown to me who fought on my behalf.

The miracle of modern medicine is not lost. I also have the great story of "happily ever after" declarative of "Kordell, you are now a cancer survivor." You want to be able to tell some stories. In a charismatic relationship, it might be said that you *must* tell others.

Humans are drawn to stories. Especially human customers. We can relate. When the mighty fall or the common person conquers, we call that entertainment. We shake our heads in disbelief. Empathy has us thinking, internalizing and associating. Charisma has the communication dial turned up all the way. It understands the power of narrative, using stories

with great abandon. The charismatic experience fits the classic
tale of tales:

- The hero is introduced.
- A journey is undertaken.
- The monster raises its snarling head.
- The hero fights and wins.
- The moral of the story is contemplated.

To connect with the customer, consider them as the hero.
Their journey confronts a monster— a problem—that you can
help them fight. For the customer's odyssey and battles, they
see your weapons as part of their journey. In business, those
are the promises of value you contribute. They want your help
but have one issue. Before they confront the dragon with you,
do you have any sort of proof? This is the classic formula of
marketing. Sometimes referred to as the
"marketing>message>method," this frame is used in
connecting with the customer. The customer wants something
they can connect with instead of the self-serving patter they get
from "vendors."

Problem (them) > **Promise** (you) > **Proof** (story)

Writes Annette Simmons in her excellent book, *The Story
Factor*:

"People don't want more information. They are up to
eyeballs in information. They want *faith*—faith in you,
your goals, your success, in the story you tell. It is faith
that moves mountains, not facts. Facts do not give birth to
faith. Faith needs a story to sustain it, a meaningful story

that inspires belief in you and renews hope that your ideas indeed offer what you promise."[20]

Stories stick. They make the difficult easy to understand. The listener can make the jump to more complex application for themselves. Again from Annette Simmons:

> "Telling a meaningful story means inspiring your listeners—coworkers, leaders, subordinates, family or a bunch of strangers—to reach the same conclusions you have reached and decided for themselves to believe what you say and do what you want them to do. *People value their own conclusions more highly than yours* (italics added). Once people make your story their story, you have tapped into the powerful force of faith. Future influence will require very little follow-up energy from you and may even expand as people recall and retell your story to others."[21]

Stories can make business run smoother. One senior executive found himself in never-ending meetings, refereeing between subordinates in their turf battles. Finally, he told them that they could not come to him until they had a solution. Now they not only brought him their troubles, but they also offered a solution that would benefit them while harming the business. He finally brought in two senior executives who were often in conflict and told the following story:

"The fire alarms blared, telling all in the manufacturing plant to quickly exit. The production folks went quickly out the back of the building where there was not much space and where they could not be accounted for. It was quick. The office personnel went out the front. When the emergency forces arrived and took a quick census, they entered the building to rescue the missing. Meanwhile, one of the fire fighters walked around the building to discover the missing people in the back. Everyone was counted. Which group was right?"

"They both were," said one of the vice presidents.

"I would suspect that both of you are correct," said the senior executive. "You both feel like your department should have the lead on this issue. I need you two to discuss this and agree on what is best for the company and for our customers."

One story made his time more effective, made decisions better, and sent a message that professionals work with each other. How do you relate to the rich, the poor, the educated, the common man? Is there a way to cross all cultures, races, and sexes? Yes, through stories. "And he taught them many things by parables"[22] If it is good enough for Him, should you not practice, manage, speak, and train in stories? A certain man falling among thieves immediately engages the hearer.

Professional speakers learn quickly that stories become the bread and butter of their profession. In fact, great presentations start with a story in the first three seconds. No more opening comments like "I am glad to be here today." Boring. Grab the audience's attention and interest now with a story.

There is a need today for "industrial strength teachers." These wizards of wisdom transport customers to a new place with stories. Their narratives make us want to engage *with* the new. Said Christopher Columbus to the monarchs of Spain, "You don't drive south and turn left. You go west. This big world is round, you see." The story reverberates with a call for exploration, of challenging the known and delving into the unknown.

So powerful are stories in business that organizations have benefited for decades . . . even if the stories are not true.

- Hertz is not number one. Enterprise is larger than Hertz and Avis combined.

- What about that flat world and Christopher Columbus? Eratosthenes calculated the circumference of the (round) earth in Egypt in 240 BC. Nevertheless, a great storyteller like Washington Irving (think Rip Van Winkle) drove a flat world story for generations.
- Washington never cut down a cherry tree.
- The panic induced by the "War of the Worlds" radio broadcast? Never happened.

However, they all make for great stories! People love stories. Stories are passed on even if they are not true. Advertising is famous for stories that "brand" themselves into the mind of the customer. "Ring around the collar" sold Wisk detergent for decades. "Winston tastes good like a cigarette should," systematically destroyed lives. Years after the advertising ended, you can ask any women what Michelin tires represent. They will reference babies sitting inside tires and comments on how Michelin will protect your little ones. The visual story connects.

What stories do logos communicate? Consider the bite in the Apple computer logo. Does that subconsciously communicate "scamp" or "trouble-maker" associated with the Garden of Eden? Who can look at a Harley-Davidson logo and not think of tough guys in leather? Their logo evokes a story of winding roads and "wind in your face" freedom.

From the capital of stories, Los Angeles, we can observe the blossoming work of Robert McKee. When he initially started offering workshops on screenwriting, McKee's attendees totaled in the single digits. Today his seminars are attended by hundreds, including 63 Academy Award winners, 164 Emmy Award winners and countless writers and directors. Alumni include Geoffrey Rush, David Bowie, Kirk Douglas, Tom

Cruise, and Steven Pressfield. McKee has consulted 20th Century Fox, Disney, MTV, and Paramount Pictures. Said he, "Stories are the creative conversion of life itself into a more powerful, clearer, more meaningful experience. They are the currency of human contact."[23]

McKee introduces the concept of the 180° change. In each movie scene, the plot changes 180°, switching from the situation at the start of the scene to a reversal at the end. The scene starts with the couple getting married and being happy but ending with divorce. The scene starts with the powerful empire-building tyrant invading and ends with his defeat and death. Consider the plot changes of the following:

- "Toto, I've got a feeling we are not in Kansas anymore."
- "Frankly, Scarlett, I don't give a damn."
- "Luke, I am your father."

Because a movie (story) can make this 180° change, it has the ability to intellectually and emotionally transport the audience (customer/employee) toward a new horizon.

Consider the story of Easy Eddie. As the lawyer for Al Capone, Easy Eddie made a lot of money. Capone stayed out of jail and Eddie's kids drove new cars. Eddie's house in Chicago occupied a whole city block. However, Easy Eddie had a communication problem. He knew that his kids *knew* where the money was coming from. He sent a message to his kids and turned over Mr. Capone's tax records to the federal government. Al Capone went to prison and Easy Eddie communicated his principles.

Two weeks before Capone's release, Easy Eddie was gunned down. Capone sent his message too. Easy Eddie had already broadcast through actions, his principles. The example of morals and ethics sealed in the blood of a martyr.

Years later, the story influences World War II. Japanese bombers were in route to the USS Lexington, when Butch took on nine planes by himself. In a solo battle, Butch used sixty rounds per bomber and dropped five from the sky while dodging enemy file. Because of his achievement, he became the first flying ace of World War II. Eighteen months later, he lost his life in combat. Would his heroics go unnoticed? His hometown made sure that would not happen, so they built monuments in his honor. In the Chicago airport sits a large display, a monument to the heroics of Butch O'Hare, for whom the airport is named. The 180° twist? Butch O'Hare was Easy Eddie's son!

What cultural values does your business communicate with its stories? David Packard (of Hewlett Packard) arrived at his office on a Saturday to find one of his employees locked out. This young worker was hoping to come in to get a jump on a big project. From that point onward, Packard made it company policy that every employee should have access to their building, even on weekends.

The Hewlett Packard story signals that employees have priority over a locked door. When charismatic businesses use stories, they inspire and motivate. Education lifts the customer and the organization's employees.

Big Hairy Audacious Concept

Like Columbus and his round world, charisma often calls on a Big Hairy Audacious Concept (BHAC). This BHAC story transports the customer to a different place. To get a BHAC you must know the customer's world. This understanding lets you communicate your value in a way so the customer sees their world in a new way. It is a real "Wow, if we do what you are proposing, it will transition us totally."

*If I had listened to my customers, they would have asked
for a faster horse.*

HENRY FORD

*People don't know what they want until you
show it to them.*

STEVE JOBS

BHAC stories are common in charismatic business: iPhones by Apple, bagless vacuum cleaners by Dyson, overnight delivery by FedEx. So many businesses have great value that could rock the customer's world, but instead you get "We are a best kept secret." Stories can negate the customer blind spots. The Greeks had a word for the blind spots—*scotomas*, that is, spots in the visual field where vision is missing. To illustrate, read the following sample sentence:

Two of the most powerful and effective of all human fears are the fear of failure and the fear of success.

Now go back, reread the sentence, and count how many times the letter "f" occurs. How many did you find? Are you sure? When we were taught to read, we were coached to "sound out the words." We sounded the word "of" and pronounced it "off." Lovingly, we were taught that the letter f in "of" has an "ov" sound (as in "love"). You become educated. Your brain was trained to convert the "f" to a "v." Education teaches the proper way to see things, inflicting us with blind spots. Did you get all eleven f's in the above sample sentence?

It is not that the customer is indifferent to your value, but that they may be conditioned with their current life map to not always comprehend your offerings. Perhaps they have to justify their decision to purchase another product. Maybe their experience has built a blind spot to the very thing they need. They just do not see the f's.

Introduce a new concept with a story and the chances of it taking root climb.

> "And the disciples came and said unto him, 'Why speakest thou unto them in parables?'
>
> He answered, 'Because it is given unto you to know the mysteries of the kingdom of heaven, but to them it is not given.'"[24]

Mysteries? In their powerful book, *The Challenger Sale*, Matthew Dixon, and Brent Adamson share:

> "Just as you can't be an effective teacher if you're not going to push your students, you can't be an effective Challenger if you're not going to push your customers. This approach is so important today with customer risk aversion as high as it is. . . . The bigger problem is that customers often fall into their buying zone when it comes to buying. . . . The Challenger moves customers out of their comfort zone by showing them their world in a different light."[25]

You become a teacher and weave a story that communicates how others traveled a certain road, ran into dragons, found success, and then applied their new insights.

The six parts of a BHAC are:

1. "Let me tell you a story about something that happened." The new idea is shared as a story. "XYZ found that they were experiencing _____."
2. Share the details, science, data, studies, and surveys that support the new idea.

3. The BHAC then expounds the challenges that others had because of this new idea. The customer starts to think, "Yes, those are the challenges that I have as well."
4. "Here are the things they did to escape/discover the new thing."
5. The customer is mentally saying, "This story is us; we are similar to this."
6. By association, they assume you can address this issue for them because you would not share the story if you could not fix things.

After James Dyson created more than 5,000 prototypes, he tried to sell his bagless invention to the leading vacuum cleaner manufacturers. They told him that he did not understand their business. Their blind spots said that they did indeed sell vacuums. However, their real business was in vacuum bags. Theirs was a "free razor to sell razor blades" model. He knew his vacuum solved the problem of those suction-losing bags. He just could not get the manufacturers to see that customers wanted suction. They had blind spots induced by the ransom they charged for bags. He needed to create his BHAC. The manufacturers were blinded with the desire to have customers buy bags *from* them in predictable transactions. He wanted customers to vacuum *with* his cyclone technology that would transform the way they cleaned. Dyson needed a compelling story while the industry needed to see things differently. The customers, meanwhile, voted for the product that gave them what they wanted—suction—while not being held hostage on purchasing bags.

While walking past the vacuum section of one retailer, I noticed that the Dyson product was three times more expensive. The knock-off brands had signs that proclaimed that they "outperform Dyson." That Dyson still sells might be a testament to lost trust in those who made the customer sacrifice for so long.

How do you get men to wear women's underwear? When athletes considered the qualities of women's undergarments, they thought, "How could we get men to take advantage of these lightweight and wicking materials?" You give them a name, a story that speaks to swords, jousting, and battle— Under Armor.

Sara Blakely relates how she took her female buyers into restrooms where she told the slimming story of Spanx with a pair of white pants. She relates her paranoia of talking to others, fearful that they would take her BHAC before she got sales of "cutting the feet out of panty hose" to get a slimming effect and then steal it.

Charismatic organizations find brilliance in the succinct story to communicate value. In table salt, the story allows a 200 to 300% higher price over the competitor's exact same product.

- "When it rains, it pours." (Morton Salt)
- "It is hard to stop a Trane."
- "Nothing runs like a Deere."

What is your story? Are you so used to how your company started that you do not share the journey anymore? Do you relate the story of how your customers found your value?

If you are a best-kept-secret, take control of the narrative. Recruit friends and advisors to help find the story. "Too close to the forest to see the trees" is a real condition. We do not see the "f's." Charisma is in the ability to motivate, lift, leverage, entertain, and make memorable your values, and your vision in stories.

What unspoken message occurs with competitors when a prominent technology company pronounces its story line, "Do no evil." Narrative is not easy. It could require serious anthological assistance. Often one of the most liberating moments for executives during strategic planning is the simple revelation from a tool known as a graphic history. When I facilitate these sessions, this visual representation of the company's story is liberating. (See www.Grove.com.)

Even at Pixar, that gold medal story organism, there is a constant battle to get past the mechanics of making movies to improve the story. When *Sesame Street* is your narrative competitor, you must step it up. Narrative is imperative! It is an essential tool to connect. Look for your industrial strength story. Oh, ye world-class teachers, unite! It will probably need some mavericks, mavens, and misfits. There must be some unconventional behavior. Our research shows that the number one quality assigned by customers to charismatic business is creativity. Onward to the chapter on creativity that comes to the eclectic.

A Parting Shot

Great stories need to age. After his run as a TV character, Jerry Seinfield went about developing a new show. It had him writing jokes and then asking for time at various comedy clubs where he could try out his new material. Documented in the film *Comedian,* the process shows the hard work that goes into becoming an overnight success.

For ten years I watched one of the best story tellers on the planet tell and re-tell his story of a man on a cell phone in an airport gate area. He has the luxury of embellishing his narrative more than a business does. His shtick is so engaging and funny that I recently watched people in tear-induced laughter at the latest telling of the story. Your story will need to be told and messaged. With each telling, the audience or customer will give you feedback and guidance. After developing their story, Pixar takes years to fine-tune it.

Chapter 6

 **E**clectic

Unconventional Behavior and Creative World of Mavericks, Mavens, and Misfits.

> *Rule for leaders: Innovate or abdicate.*
> *Rule for companies: Innovate or evaporate.*
> BOB HEINZ

Creativity is required, and it is found in teams of individuals who are encouraged by leaders to open up a fire hose of innovation. The common sense and wisdom of groups whose members are focused on service and lifting others is a thing of dread to the competition. To the customer it is inspiring, like an army with shining banners.

Creativity and innovation put panic into traditional status quo management. "Eclectic" prompts a hiss and a put-down. Unconventional has always been hard to control and can easily be assigned to backwater stations. To satisfy customers requires trust in others, giving resources and worrying about the liabilities of bad decisions by a maverick here or there.

Creativity and charisma require real listening with heart and soul to another. True empathy allows us to see the world through others' eyes and to discover perspectives and insights missed. Business schools teach of demographics and market share while the misfits are kicking down doors to real customers with real money because they push on the rules and cause a little trouble. Why shouldn't man be able to fly? Who says you can't put a fully functional computer into a device that doubles as a phone? Who says you cannot get people to spend the

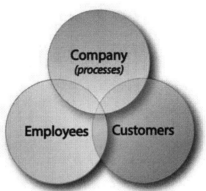

equivalent of a small car to take their kids to Florida so they can have their pictures taken with imaginary characters? These people are crazy—mavericks, mavens and misfits. Name-calling them with maverick, maven, or misfit with a snarled lip will surely get them to fall back into line and carry the company mantra like a good lemming.

These enemies of creativity say, "We have always done it this way" or "You don't understand. We tried that once and it didn't work."

Charisma, that special connection and value given my customers must pass through the door of creativity. Charisma must listen with expectations that good things will come out of service to employees, customers and the company.

The management of creativity demands that you teach and encourage innovation by employees, while being aware of the needs of the organization and its processes. There are three lenses: employees, customers, and organization (and its processes). You must have all three to have true innovation. To create without considering the company is like some goose and golden egg scenario.

To watch the work of your mavens and mavericks as they create is both educational and edifying, like watching an artist whose brush strokes turn plain canvas into a masterpiece. Watching him present, you probably would not label Kenneth Cole as the most charismatic person in the world. He is, however, a maverick. This titan of the fashion industry, with his boyish good looks and razor sharp intellect, does not come across as the example of an orator. Still, his unconventional behavior and artistic touch are reflected in the Kenneth Cole Production Company. That's right, *Production Company.*

During the beginning of his career, Cole arranged to use the equipment and facilities of the finest Italian shoe factories and craftsmen during the fallow night hours. There he churned out an inventory of top quality shoes. At the time, New York was the destination for an event called Market Week for those who buy and sell shoes. The Hilton Hotel in Manhattan was at the center of Market Week. Shoe manufacturers transformed the Hilton into an expensive show room, with whole floors taken at times by each company.

When Kenneth Cole spent all his savings building the shoes, financing hotel space was not in the sole. So, Cole asked a friend if he could borrow a semi-truck with trailer. "Ken, the city of New York will not let you park a semi on the street in front of the hotel. The only organizations that get that privilege are utility companies and movie productions." At the time New York had an initiative called "Love New York" that incentivized movie-making in the Big Apple.

Our intrepid entrepreneur changed the name of his company to Kenneth Cole Productions. Parked outside the hotel sat a semi-trailer with a massive sign announcing the "In Production" movie *The Birth of a Shoe Company*. Behind the trailer were stanchions fitted with velvet rope, complete with "actresses" and city-provided police to "keep the crowds in check." Curious shoe buyers on their way to the Hilton stopped and were ushered into the trailer only to become part of the magic of a real world movie. In a matter of days, the entire inventory of the very fashionable Kenneth Cole *Production* was sold out. Cole is a maverick.

Being eclectic seeds the coming charisma. Look at the unconventional behavior on a macro scale of a Magic Kingdom dream. On a micro scale, it does something as unconventional as actually listening to others. The eclecticism in organizations is personified in their mavericks, mavens, and misfits. This unconventional tendency turns magic into developing significance. Listen to others? How radical is that? When you consider input from others, things can get messy. If you consider that these "others" might have something of value, then the innovative insight might make you stand out. The individual creative genius of Edison might be found in a few selected individuals, but for every gifted Mozart, innovation is more commonly found in group wisdom. Whether from individuals or teams of innovators (Steve Job's Apple, for example), *unconventionality is a sine qua non to becoming charismatic.*

Our research indicates *the number one quality that determines business charisma is creativity.* In the surveys, we did not differentiate between the creativity of Disney and Victoria's Secret. Regardless of specific businesses, the participants looked at their top choices and assigned what they felt most contributed to feeling charismatic.

Being creative and eclectic will rub against the status quo. It also scares the bejeebies out of most managers. With creativity the call of the day, leadership must look for and reward the unconventional. Unless the culture can deal with the fear that comes with the unknown—that indefinable possibility—then creativity will get a stake through its heart. Charismatic companies celebrate the iconoclastic behaviors that fuel innovation. They challenge the enemy in times of war and the home office in times of peace. Ted Hoff's microprocessor jet fueled at a little startup called Intel. Steve Wozniak, working night hours in his HP cubicle, created an Apple of a product. Street sweepers at Disney really think that they ought to be cartoon artists with their straw brooms on the concrete "canvas" sidewalks.

The processes of business constitute a real equity. Organizations must champion innovation into the processes. Those who control the processes with budgetary discretion must become aware of how they can grow innovation. Why? The line manager gets a degree of controlling power from the ability to say "No." The nature of creativity, however, is to bust loose from the status quo with an exploring and curious "Yes."

The research shows that is hard to find business charisma in control industries like banks, accounting firms, architects, engineering entities and health care. Yet the biggest opportunity is in these industries. Consider the recent revolution in training doctors. Some medical schools are putting doctorate students through Emergency Medical Technicians (EMT) training as a first step in their medical school. Give the future doctors firsthand experience in the trauma of real-world medical emergencies. A senior executive (and one of my clients) has to fire a doctor every now and then to send the message that bedside manners matter more than ego.

Bedside manners can literally be life or death. The "controlling things" discussion pulls down creativity with the ongoing debate asking, "Does clinical expertise trump bedside manners?" How creative do you want the banker to be with your money? This is not the brand of creativity found in charisma. The creativity the customer is looking for comes in ways to help them advance and succeed. They can tell when partnership is replaced by "me-manship."

Airlines and cable companies struggle with this. The planes must land safely. The internet must stay "up" 24/7. They want the customer to give and then brainstorm new ways to get more. The value does not go up. The interests of the customer are missing. They want the customer to come to their altar of business and offer up their checkbook. Wring out a little more, and then repeat.

Customer sacrifice is about wringing every dollar from the customer. The non-charismatic businesses justify this practice. Kill the golden goose so we can have our pâté today. Never mind the golden eggs. Southwest Airlines maintained a steady upward trajectory when they fought against the customer sacrifice-oriented competitors. Will they continue as they think more like managers and less like leaders? Talk to their flight crews, and the message is starting to creep in that a different organization is taking shape. Are they changing from a transportation company (in their early days they suggested that they were an alternative to taking the bus) to be a traditional airline?

A business that makes nothing but money is a poor kind of business.

HENRY FORD

Creativity is providing value that transforms the customer's world. The customers vote with dollars for those who understand the notion of charisma. In the life-altering relationship, they reward. Creativity must be a serious practice.

Will you get it right? Not always. Is that not why we practice? Talk to your customer, listen, and then act. Like the parent lecturing the child, you too might miss the connecting moments. Recognized too late, you cannot go back, especially as you watch the tail lights of passing competition.

Humor = Tragedy + Time.

This charisma stuff can be funny. Charisma and humor are like salt and pepper—a real Laurel and Hardy pair. One seems to tag along with the other. Of special note is the general tendency for humor and creativity to cohabit. Humor is often the unexpected, the creative surprise, the twist, or last minute turn. When referencing then President Jimmy Carter's bungling brother, Billy, Johnny Carson said, "I don't mind people shooting themselves in the foot, but the problem with Billy is that he can reload so fast."

Unlike the ironic editorial content of a Scott Adams "Dilbert" comic strip, charisma finds good-hearted humor essential. Sarcasm rarely qualifies as a building block. The boss who is more humorous is respected more by their followers, is more effective, and better at coaching. In like manner, organizations that do not take themselves too seriously create entertainment and laughter that are magnetic. That self-deprecating humor creates humility and humanity. The customer just assumes that you are having a good time, and so they should. Might it also hint of improvement?

If the script is set, that is, never to change, then the ongoing creativity ceases. The Jungle Cruise in the Magic Kingdom has over twenty iterations of their spiel with more to come for sure. Southwest Airlines is famous for the creativity they give to their flight attendants. On one flight the flight attendants pointed out that the overhead bins "are for your large pieces of luggage, small children, or unruly husbands."

The long hallway waiting line for the Muppet's 4D adventure at a Disney park entertains with humorous titles on office doors:

DEPARTMENT OF MAKING THING$ MORE
EXPENSIVE THAN WE CAN AFFORD

STRESS TESTING DEPARTMENT. CAUTION!
CONTENTS UNDER EXTREME PRESSURE

One hallway brick arch has a large missing chunk of brick with a small lettered sign proclaiming "ouch." Who takes a beautiful arch and then whacks a chunk out of it? Instead of punishing the class clown, charisma celebrates the unconventional behavior. Wanted: Mavens, Misfits, and Mavericks. Heck, let's celebrate the comedians as well. Warning: It takes a confidant leadership team to manage and coax the egos and personalities of their eclectics.

A Call for Five Humans and an Accountant.
There is wisdom in groups. Charismatic organizations celebrate the latent abilities and intelligence of their workers. Expect trouble relying on the brilliance of one individual here and another there. Trends come too fast. The value of a network of non-biased vendors, customers, and other stakeholders is necessary.

So if products can be customized and delivered in mass, how do you differentiate?

"If we all got together and honestly confessed our sins to each other, we would die of laughter because of a lack of originality."

MICHAEL VANCE

Creativity and innovation should be on the program right after the opening hymn. Then the self-doubt that comes with creating second thoughts produces a fog. The fear of losing control stalks creativity, often calling for the comforting "proven." Research and crunching numbers can put creativity into recess. The fairy dust of charisma is that it is not on the well-traveled road. Drummed into the mind of every breathing member of *Homo sapiens* is healthy respect (and fear) for the unknown. That dark forest surely has claws and teeth that will eat you.

One way to eliminate the beast is to study those who traveled the road previously. C.A.S.E. (Copy and Steal Everything) is a two-edge sword. By copying too closely, the work of others will make your work feel derivative. To ignore the maps of those who have gone before is foolish. Once the research is finished, the creative people "shut the books" and moves on. How many rewrites will you do after you read the next book? *Done is better than perfect.*

The rewards are too great to be ignored. "If we continue to do what we have always done, then we will continue to get what we have always gotten." The following books can be considered essential reading: *The War of Art* by Pressfield, *Creativity Inc.* by Catmull, or *Steal Like an Artist* by Kleon. The fears of creativity and innovation scream for industrial strength courage. "What if this course has a waterfall into oblivion at the course end?"

Robert Frost so captured the fear in the following selected stanzas:

Two roads diverged in a yellow wood,
And sorry I could not travel both
And be one traveler, long I stood
And looked down one as far as I could
To where it bent in the undergrowth;

I shall be telling this with a sigh
Somewhere ages and ages hence:
Two roads diverged in a wood, and I—
I took the one less traveled by,
And that has made all the difference.[26]

A poet would know this torment of creativity. Consider Shakespeare's take:

There is a tide in the affairs of men.
Which, taken at the flood, leads on to fortune;
Omitted, all the voyage of their life
Is bound in shallows and in miseries.
On such a full sea are we now afloat,
And we must take the current when it serves,
Or lose our ventures.[27]

The fear of the untested, the untried, is what keeps the competition at bay. Dread keeps the rivals comfortably harbored with safe, proven efforts. The bigger the enterprise, the bigger the risk. Charisma, that universe-changing prize requires more. The maverick knows that when fear kicks in, systems must push you forward. Making the decision on Monday expects a Friday course correction.

". . . Early on, all of our movies suck," says Ed Catmull in his book, *Creativity, Inc.* "To pursue such an insane goal of having rats prepare food (ratatouille) or to have almost forty minutes of no dialog to open a movie (*WALL-E*) requires nerves of steel."

"If you want to get into a great college, you need to write a certain way," says the teacher to the high school student. Year after year, the invisible learning is programmed into the next generation. The innocent and childlike qualities of play, laughter, and spontaneity are diluted down with a more educated mind. Education studies history so it is "not repeated." This makes for generals who struggle with preparation for the next battle as they study the last war. Education then prepares a generation to fight a land war when the next battle will occur on sea.

"Oh, but if we get a great leader, they will guide us safely there." Most likely, that leader, if they do indeed guide the ship, will do the unconventional. The winner has adaptability to be creative or to glean the wisdom and insights of groups. Gleaning creativity is hard work. High performance only comes from 20% of your teams. Beware the call for "glory to the silos and kingdom building!" Not today, thank you.

To drive creativity, there must be a culture that encourages the maverick, maven, and misfit. It is a lot easier to manage the average than to give rope to the top outlier employee. Culture must understand the sheer panic of striking out on untried paths.

I once managed a team of technology sales people. Their productivity had been consistently improving. Then a true maverick joined the team. He immediately brought opportunities that were double the size of the combined sales of the rest of the team. His focus was on customer problems beyond our comfort zone. His sales were way outside normal business parameters. I found myself having conversations with the CEO and Chairman of the Board, each who had to consider banking covenants and financial models that were new. The maverick was as much work as the other seven sales people combined. The rest of the team, however, was watching. "Hey, we can do that too." The multiplying effect of one person's creativity proved infectious to others.

There must be a system to identify the obstacle and then apply seeds of creativity. This system pushes the innovation forward where it can be refined, enhanced, debugged, championed, and executed.

It takes nerves of steel to create and support a culture for creativity. This is where smaller, nimble competitors take advantage. Compare Dyson to Hoover, Microsoft to IBM.

"My dad can beat up your dad." At the core of anti-charisma is the philosophy that you do not need good road manners if you are a five-ton truck. If you are the biggest gorilla, then you always win. "*I* am awesome because *I* am faster, bigger, and better." "*We* need to be feared." Such language focuses on the past and present. The second person "you" and "your" tend to be future oriented. A "you will be able to" transport subjects to the unknown of tomorrow.

Malcolm Gladwell's insightful tome, *David and Goliath: Underdogs, Misfits and the Art of Battling Giants*, smacks the misguided religion of bigger is better in the forehead with an innovation rock. While the leaders of the day were offering David armor, swords, and shields, he rightly responded, "No thank you, just let me stop and get a little boulder." Was the charismatic David savvy about the proven tools of warfare, or did he just have a naïve belief in his own skills and talents?

Charismatic organizations know that their very existence depends on the creativity and innovation of their employees. Their soldiers are the troops in the trenches who think outside of the proverbial box because they know what the competition is doing. They also know what "we are not doing."

In the early days of Southwest Airlines, the company experienced operating losses. The decision was to sell 25% of Southwest's fleet—one airplane. The employees could see there might be a decrease in headcount. They partitioned Herb Kelleher, the charismatic leader of Southwest, to let them keep staffing to make the three planes do the work of four. They proposed a gate turnaround of ten minutes. At the time, it took an hour to get passengers off, clean the plane, stock the food, and drink for the next flight, and to load passengers for the next trip. If the sixty-minute turnaround could be done in ten minutes, more flights could occur and the current employees would be needed.

How do you do the impossible? Instead of a cleaning crew boarding the plan, the flight attendants started at the back of the plane and cleaned as passengers disembarked. Pilots loaded luggage. Tickets were gathered on the plane. Kelleher couldn't create that kind of urgency. He certainly would not suggest those demands of his employees. They—the employees—had to think unconventionally.

Our natural tendency is to study our perceived Goliaths. We think that big and bad will ensure that no one will mess with us. That is just one strategy, and charismatic organizations often use one of the other four strategies. Remember, it is about unconventional behavior. The water skiing boat is quicker than the oil tanker, more responsive to shifts in current and the interests of the customer.

The Five Strategies

"I am the biggest" is a strategy. It is the most used and most prone to failure. Sears, General Motors, Kodak, and a non-stop churn of titans tumble to the unconventional attack of smaller, more creative competition. If your door is big enough, no one can kick it down. Therefore, we will use that analogy and title it that way.

What are the other strategies for battle? How much charisma does it take to be the biggest? What are other, more unconventional strategies?

1. Door Kicker
2. Create and Contrarian
3. End-Around
4. Divide and Conquer
5. FUD

Door Kicker Strategy

Being the biggest is tough stuff. Everyone else is shooting at you. Your work is cut out, as others believe that biggest is best, and so you become the target. AT&T was broken up into the "baby bells" by court order and resulting value of the RBOCs (Regional Bell Operating Companies). These smaller, more nimble entities had huge returns for shareholders. On the other hand, IBM fended off a government attack on their size only to trudge into a long press of mediocrity. It took an unconventional Lou Gerstner to shake Big Blue out of their hypnotic state.

When you are Babylon, with your five-mile long walls spanning the mighty Euphrates River, allowing a non-quenchable source of water, you are the biggest, baddest kid on the block. Those walls were wide enough for chariots to turn around on (up to one hundred feet wide), and estimates put the height at places of up to three hundred feet tall. How do you kick in the door on something that big? "We are Sears. Hear us roar."

In the classic movie, *The Princess Bride*, Vizzini shares classic insight into this strategy:

Vizzini: "… Ha ha! You fool! You fell victim to one of the classic blunders, the most famous of which is 'Never get involved in a land war in Asia.' But only slightly less well-known is this: 'Never go in against a Sicilian when death is on the line!' Ha ha!'"

Moral of the story: If you are as big as Asia, no one is going to be fool enough to take you down. Are they?

Create and Contrarian Strategy

Clayton Christensen's book, *Innovator's Dilemma*, suggests that there is always something new in the wings. Michael Vance, that classic thinker on creativity, postured early in his career that there are three types of creativity (he later added to these). For simplification, they are:

- Invention - Invention - aka - the bomb
- Invention - Extension - a bomb with a rocket under it
- Invention - Devention - how do you "devent" a nuclear missile?

Or

- Invention – Invention . . . a pencil.
- Invention – Extension . . . a mechanical pencil.
- Invention – De-vention . . . an eraser.

To create, to bring about the new or rearrange the old in new ways, requires contrarian thinking. By its very nature, creativity distances you from the competition. When you see price wars, you are seeing the lack of creativity. "Since I look and smell like everyone else, then the one thing that differentiates is the lowest price." When you have to sell on price, then you will always sell on price until you become creative and unconventional. Take it from yours truly. I was in the middle of the no-name generic food revolution of the late 1970s.

I can create faster than they can copy.

WALT DISNEY

End-around Strategy

Cyrus, the ancient Iranian king, looked up at the massive walls of Babylon, scanned the surrounding terrain, and told his men, "We need to rock this place." No frontal attacks, no *mano a mano* strategies here. Cyrus and his mighty army dammed the mighty Euphrates and walked into Babylon under the walls on the riverbed.

Reed Hastings saw the rented video tape slide out from under the car seat and had that sickening feeling of "Uh, oh. I wonder how big the late charges are going to be on that monster? Why can't I rent video tapes like my gym membership, so much a month for unlimited use?" Instead of competing with a Babylon (like Blockbuster Video) with it hundreds of stores, Hastings did a creative end-around and got into the customer's home fortress through the mailbox. Netflix marches into the city under the walls.

Divide and Conquer Strategy

Hertz is number one in rental cars, with Avis trying harder to catch up. Meanwhile, the charismatic rental company that "delivers to your home" pursued a subset of the market. Enterprise went after those who needed a replacement car. That is how they started. They sliced off a piece of the market. At this writing, Enterprise is larger than Hertz and Avis combined. That didn't happen just because they focused on the broken vehicle or insurance market. They seriously train their employees in customer service, giving them huge freedoms to go beyond customer expectations.

This customer-centric focus is reinforced by participation in a Net Promoter Score, a system that places customers into three groups: detractors, passives, and promoters. Take the percentage of customers who are promoters and subtract the detractors and you have your score. Remember that a quality of charisma is that it creates champions, those promoters that testify of their membership in the fan club.

A look at organizations on the Net Promoter Scoreboard and you will almost see a match with our business charisma companies. Jerry Murrell and his five sons (guys) started making hamburgers with the best quality ingredients they could find. They went after a market that loved quality hamburgers like those that you would cook at home. In his first Five Guys Hamburgers and Fries, the customers balked at the high price. Jerry told them, "Try it, and if you don't like it, then the burger is on me." Customers accepted his challenge and forked over the cash. What a novel approach—make a straightforward product that is better than the competition. The audacity, the horror. Way to go, Five Guys. It gives new meaning to the phrase *value meal*.

A special note on Five Guys. Murrell, a former financial planner, suggested they could save a lot of money by just putting one tomato slice on the hamburger. His five guys (sons) revolted. Instead, they raised prices to reflect the higher food costs. Charisma is giving the customer a product that cannot be replaced. One tomato slice? You can get that at the competent, average burger joint down the street. Five Guys sticks to what makes them creative and innovative. They go after the market that wants the unique product, which happens to be food that tastes great because of quality ingredients.

Yet, knowledge is not enough. In a moment of forgetfulness, the educated laboratory technician who can discover the presence of cholera in the water supply, drinks and dies.

Wisdom is the application of knowledge. Wisdom would warn, as Vizzini did, to "never get involved in a land war in Asia." Wisdom divides and conquers.

FUD Strategy

FUD stands for Fear, Uncertainty, and Doubt. It is the process used by big business to discredit others. In the technology sector both IBM and Microsoft used it for years. Why does Google's phrase of "do no evil" resonate with the technology world? Might it be a grenade toss at the champions of FUD, as if to ask with a grimace, "Do you *really* want to buy that product?" With a wink, wink they say, "It is interesting that you would buy something like *that*, because it will be outdated quickly. We are coming out with something better shortly, and you will be glad you waited."

I think this strategy has long-term, negative implications for anyone who uses it. It does not take long to realize that those who use it are bullies, and no one likes a bully. The charismatic organization lifts and contributes; they do not tear down. Our surveys did not find any organization that used this strategy to win.

Tools for Creativity

Brainstorming

This often-misunderstood practice falls behind the shadow of a bigger focus of decision making. Since the number one characteristic assigned as charismatic is creativity, improving brainstorming is fundamental.

The Nine Rules of Brainstorming:

1) Brainstorming is a timed process.
2) You need at least one, if not more recorders.
3) There is no criticism or judgment of ideas.
4) Wild and Wooly ideas are welcome.

5) No one works from notes.
6) The more ideas the better.
7) Hitchhike off one another's ideas.
8) It is not done "off site."
9) The boss goes last.

Brainstorming Is a Timed Process.

There is a reason for scoreboards. Bowling without watching the pins drop just does not work. Deadlines awaken the human spirit and mind. By limiting time and keeping score, the excitement level goes up in a competition of thinking.

You Need at Least One if not More Recorders.

Ideas will come fast. Designate someone with decent handwriting who can keep up and not judge as brainstormers generate ideas. Instruct them to collect both the initial idea *and* the follow-along ideas that are enhancements. If two people are recording, tell them to not to worry about duplicating; you can sort that out after the fur stops flying. Quantity is more important than quality at this point. Recording tricks like abbreviations, acronyms, misspelled words are encouraged. What good is creativity if you cannot discover a new way to spell a word?

There Is No Criticism or Judgment of Ideas.

Great brainstorming groups are made of five humans and an accountant. There is nothing wrong with the analytic accountant, engineer, or quality control person. However, when the analytic brings the creative process to a halt with their judgments and comments, then the free flow of brainstorming ceases.

Wild and Wooly Ideas Are Welcome.

Since no judgment is done during brainstorming, the wild, grandiose, and nonsensical ideas might seem silly. Out of the silly, however, come serious paradigm shifts and epiphanies in direction. Turn street sweepers into cartoon artists (Disney). Attach a personal computer to your belt (iPhone). Mount a floor vacuum to the wall to dry hands (Dyson). Part of the energy of brainstorming is the freedom that comes with escape from the mature mind.

The More Ideas the Better.

The tension that a contest creates pushes the collective. How high can the score go? To push out ideas will get everyone in the group participating. Individual strengths and perspectives are all up for consideration in the chase for diverse thinking

Hitchhike off Fellow Brainstorming Team Members

Suppose the subject is "how do we make a bathroom better?" One brainstorm participant might say, "Incorporate design that allows for dirty laundry as one steps out of their clothes." Another brainstormer hitchhikes off an idea with, "Perhaps have a trap door at the base of the shower/tub where you drop your clothes and then nudge them into a receiving pipe where they are whisked away—all with your foot." The synergy that comes from the iconoclast and different backgrounds sparks ideas into a full forest blaze. One of the beauties of brainstorming is stacking ideas on top of one another.

No One Works from Notes

As soon as someone starts reading from their notes, then manners and politeness naturally stop contributing. We are naturally inclined to respect others who have "thought things out."

It Is not Done Off-site.

If the only time people get creative is when they are away from the office, then innovation is held hostage until the next time a retreat is budgeted. Encourage everyone to brainstorm solutions real time. Don't complain; do something about it instead.

The Boss Goes Last

In most cases, when the boss gives ideas, culture takes over and people stop contributing. "She is the boss, after all," they say, so the thinking goes making her the smartest cookie in the room. "That is what my paycheck says." Yes, her idea may be great, but people tend to shut down in reverence and respect for position. Especially watch out for a boss who would break the third rule of not evaluating ideas. If the supervisor is critical, then shoot the innovation hoped for in the face. Too graphic? Not at all.

Idea Enhancing Questions

Information is so readily available that creativity might best be found not by the answers but by the questions asked. As provocateur, a list of questions might spark to life new thinking. Use the list below with a brainstorming session when you want to excite ideas.

- How did this problem come about? Did another problem create this one?
- How could we make this problem worse?
- Who owns this problem? Who could own it? Who should own it?
- What happens if we make it smaller in size? Bigger in size?
- What happens after this problem occurs? Might it be better to let the problem occur later?
- Who can help us address this problem? Who would help us look differently at this problem? Why?
- What does my heart and emotions tell me about this problem?
- How would great entrepreneurs like Steve Jobs or Richard Branson attack this

problem?
- If the solution created complete failure in addressing the problem, what would we learn?
- If the problem is broken down into individual components, which would be the one where creativity would most impact? Why? How?
- What are the results that occur because of this problem? Can we change the results?
  - What are the assumptions about the problem? What if I changed those?
  - Who helps clarify the problem? What aspects of the problem would they focus on?
  - If we created a fix for the problem, who would see value in it? What would they value specifically?

The Power of "Backcasting."

Who can predict the future? Care to prophesy about your world twenty-four months from now? Then consider "backcasting." Used with brainstorming, a group is told they have been time traveling to some future point. This is, of course, a mental exercise. On that future calendar, the brainstorming participants are interviewed for a documentary on the success of time between the present day and the future. "What caused your great success? What did you do to change your outcomes? What obvious things did you focus on that brought about results so quickly?"

With "predict the future" blocking removed, the mind easily focuses on the possibility from the hindsight perspective of backcasting.

Rome Was Not Built in a Nanosecond.

How can you innovate unless you have assessed the environment? Surveys, audits, focus groups, and the like are constant. It all started with a product called the Ballbarrow. James Dyson had a near face-plant in his backyard when his wheelbarrow's front wheel sunk into a mud puddle. Ever the eclectic, he went ahead to build his version of the wheelbarrow with the front wheel replaced with a large ball. The Ballbarrow was born.

During the life of the Ballbarrow, Dyson observed a large industrial machine outside a building for moving waste. This cyclonic device sucked sawdust from inside the building to an outside container, then to be hauled off.

He wondered if he could apply that same technology to a vacuum. The vacuum he had recently purchased sucked because it did not suck. Five thousand iterations later, the charismatic Dyson Vacuum with its bagless cyclone technology sprang to life. Along the way, the leading manufacturers, stuck in their offices and rationalizing and plotting the gain of respective market share, did not see the creative and disruptive arrival.

The demise of vacuum bags was the equivalent of a trip to the hardware store. Get outside of your day-to-day environment and ask, "How could this thing help me be more effective?" Field trips to the store, mall, Disney business and the library can be a major source of fuel for creativity. When your only tool is a hammer, then all problems look like nails. To get new creativity tools requires a recess break.

We humans appropriate too often. Safe is too comfortable. It creates analysis paralysis. A friend who works at a large institutionalized university commented on the tendency to think that all great ideas were found at his school. He said that they were slow to create. "We are so slow that ivy grows on us." Pixar sends artists on field trips for new perspectives on how things work, what they look like, how materials behave. Says Pixar's Ed Catmull: "Anything less is derivative."

What sustains a business is its values and processes. The resources assigned for values and processes are controlled by politics, market potential, and current budgets. Divisions, kingdoms, and departmental "silos" make sure that "the wheels stay on the cart." Their agenda eventually makes the customer feel like they are there to support the business instead of the businesses engaging and delighting them.

What about failure? Unconventional behavior can make for an easy target for those who are concerned with appearances and jealous pursuit of power. Fanning the ego will crush charisma. Steve Jobs built the next computer based on his reputation and industry standing. Charles Land had his SX-70 camera. The culture must be checked to celebrate the failure. To learn from failure sets the celebration of creativity. Today's failures become the foundation for future castles. Failing is the building block for tomorrow. It is the tomorrows that are the next element of charisma, that of time travel.

 A Parting Shot

Theodore Levitt of Harvard posited an expanding offerings model. The 1.) **Generic** product expands to the 2.) **Expected** product, which grows into the 3.) **Augmented** product. Ultimately the customer discovers the 4.) **Potential** product. Each higher level allows for differentiation and the opportunity to connect in deeper ways with the customer. When industry norms are set for service, warranties, prices, or customer relations then the obvious direction is to move to higher levels. To do this your employees can help with a **Plus 1**. Whatever the customer is expecting as a standard, you will have to add a Plus 1. If they expect paper bags you Plus 1 and give them plastic. If they expect the outside of the car washed, you open the door and wash the inside of the windows. If they expect courteous service, you Plus 1 their "Thank you" with "My pleasure." These Plus 1's can be done by others. They need not cost you a lot. One thousand employees each doing a Plus 1 make the competition evaporate.

Chapter 7

Time Travel

Every Day is Monday for Those Who Lack Vision

My favorite things in life don't cost any money.
It's really clear that the most precious resource
we all have is time.

STEVE JOBS

"What makes Harley-Davidson so charismatic?" I ask.

A slight smile comes across the face of the senior executive of a large franchise chain of fast-food restaurants. "It's the sound, he says. "Maybe it's a midlife crisis that gets customers to pay ten thousand dollars more for the Harley-Davidson logo on the gas tank. Maybe it's the freedom—how it takes us back to days when we were more carefree. Perhaps we just want to be a little mischievous."

In Milwaukee, Wisconsin, stands the chrome and polish of the Harley-Davidson Museum. Across the street from the museum is a retail outlet for this storied icon. "More often than you would imagine, we see bikers in front of the museum get off, kneel, and kiss the ground," one shop employee tells me. So does Harley-Davidson sell motorcycles? Perhaps they are a social statement for biker dudes who have an alter ego to dress in leather. Harley-Davidson is about time travel. "What we sell is the ability for a forty-three-year-old accountant to dress in black leather, ride through small towns, and have people be afraid of him," explained Richard Teerlink, former President and CEO of Harley-Davidson.

Charisma has a time travel aspect. Charisma victims want to be taken to a different time. Customers buy the future. They long for the romance of the past. They are attracted to the *vision* of a different time. There are also other terms for time travel, like entertainment, education, or life-changing experiences. The business terms for time travel are more conservative: vision, mission, objectives, Key Performance Indicators (KPIs), and a host of other terms.

The day before Valentine's Day is the busiest day of the year at Victoria's Secret. It's the day when men frequent their local Victoria's Secret store. What do they know about women's foundational wear? Nothing. Victoria's Secret, one of the organizations in the top 15 of charismatic businesses, knows that they must train their employees on how to deal with these different customers—keep the dream alive while trying to deal with reality. While experts in fit and comfort for women, employees must learn how to deal with a different type of customer—men. When he says he has nothing to wear, it means he needs to do laundry. When she says she has nothing to wear, it means she does not have anything new to wear to that future event. Victoria's Secret transformed the category of women's foundations when they infused with similar perspectives to those of high fashion. The brand came into the main stream as fashion underwear in what may be the most intimate of customer relationships.

Education, that process of learning by traveling to the past, can be charismatic. In Gettysburg, Pennsylvania, there is a local tourism staple called a Staff Ride. Teams of corporate executives arrive and meet a local "expert" on the battlefield of Gettysburg. The group is escorted around the battleground while the expert educates with a narrative of the Civil War military leaders. The skirmishes and movements of armies are considered. At one stop, the story may focus on the lack of communication in battle. The question is posed, "How is this issue affecting your business right now?" The group's current obstacles are discussed and then related to the best possible solutions based on learning from battle of Gettysburg. These are lessons learned against the backstop of a common educational event. The time travel "tourist" takes the application of the past against their goals today. Narrative meets time. People are starving for those who can help them see the past or future, what that is, or how to get to it.

> *Where there is no vision, the people perish.*
> (PROVERBS 29:18)

It is like the old joke:

> **Interviewer**: "If you got this job as a rail yard switchman and looked up to see a train barreling down the main track at 50 miles an hour, and then turned and saw another train racing toward the first from the opposite direction at 60 miles an hour on the same track, what would you do?"
> **Applicant**: "I would go get my cousin Earl?"
> **Interviewer**: "Earl? Why would you go get Earl?"
> **Applicant**: "Cause he ain't never seen a train wreck fore."

The ability to time travel is so special that we study the escapades of those who do it well. Consider books on Steve Jobs, Thomas Edison, Ronald Reagan, and Jack Welch. When the Beatles exploded onto the music scene, they were the misfits of the day. Their long hair was an incredible revolution in the average home. Decades later, Beatles T-shirts are badges for those who want time travel to a safer day. "All you need is love . . . love is you we need."

The inability to time travel also provides a great deal of entertainment. The person who says it can't be done must get out of the way of those who are already doing it.

I don't understand how Apple could ruin the record business in one year on the Mac.

DOUG MORRIS
Head of Universal Music
Commenting on the new thing: iTunes

There is no reason anyone would want a computer in their home.

KEN OLSON
President and Founder of Digital Equipment Corp.
1977

Everything that can be invented has been invented.

CHARLES H. DUELL
Commissioner, U.S. Office of Patents
1899

During the first twenty years of the Personal Computer, obsolescence occurred on a monthly basis. During this time, Dell Computers built a direct sales model they sold directly to the end user. They were tearing the established resellers of PCs to shreds. The financial numbers put Dell as the place to be and their stock price soared. How do you compete with the low-cost distribution model that has cash "float" of upfront payment on credit cards, building the product, shipping it, and then paying your suppliers thirty to sixty days later?

The answer might be to increase your spending on distribution in the face of the Dell juggernaut. When the industry was racing to lower their costs, the eclectic Steve Jobs invested in retail stores. Just ten years earlier, PC resellers had closed their stores to cut costs. How foolish Jobs looked.

Although the data will change with time, a general snapshot on the outcome is revealing. In the prime years of Steve Jobs, department stores in regional malls had average sales per square foot of about $340.00. The specialty shops like those at Caesars Palace in Las Vegas had high sales per square foot. They were getting about $1,300 per square foot. Apple Computer stores during the same time were raking in $6,050 per square foot. Vive le difference.

The Three Columns

Take out a piece of paper and draw three columns.

In the first column list your qualifications, those things that make you valuable—your education achievements, years of experience, how many employees you have, the number of years you have been in business.

In the second column list the ways you deliver your value. Do you have a website? What about manufacturing plants, retail space, trucks, marketing materials, value-laden products, and even employees? List your methods of value delivery.

In the third column, list the results that your customers get because of columns one and two. What benefits do the customer see because of their relationship with you (column 1) and your business (column 2)?

The unanimous answer is column 3. The customer has a passing interest in your qualifications. They also have a passing interest in your historical capabilities (column 1).

What they really want is what *they really want*. They want someone to take them to the future . . . their future.

Column 1 represents the past, column 2 the present, and column 3 the future. Charisma understands the value of time travel.

> *If I had listened to the customer, I would have built a faster horse.*
>
> HENRY FORD

> *The customer doesn't know what they want until I show it to them.*
>
> STEVE JOBS

The charismatic business and its leader are valued for their ability to inspire and deliver a future value. JFK did this as president when he said, "By the end of this decade we will put a man on the moon."

Disney understands this with their EPCOT Center (or Experimental Prototype Community of Tomorrow) which is dedicated to the future. Why can you find grandparents in the Magic Kingdom? Might they be going back in time for memories going forward? What? Apple communicated time travel in "a world without limits." What about "a long, long time ago in a galaxy far away." Did *Star Wars* trumpet time-travel charisma? Note that Disney digested *Star Wars* into their business. Do the Disney folks understand something you might be overlooking?

There is no better time to take the customer to the future than right now. Time is the new currency of business. The charismatic takes these past and future states and capitalizes on them right now. As a species, we humans spend 95% of our mental time in the past and future. The fears of the future and re-living our past defeats or successes have us mentally anywhere but here. The charismatic understand that keeping people in the present is essential. We count those who help us focus on the *right now* as providing a service. Consider the customer service person focused on policies and procedures that repeatedly make a bad situation worst. I ordered a simple replacement part for my car. I then experienced the wrong part ordered six times before I appealed to the owner of the franchise. He then chalked up another mistake by ordering the wrong part once again.

Research showed that in the past a bad experience was shared with twenty-six friends and acquaintances. Today the jilted customers post on social networks to tens of thousands. In today's world of Yelp, Rotten Tomatoes, and Facebook, these mistakes are magnified.

The customer can clearly see when you are not focused on them right now. Clock watching by your cast members will cause them to miss being in the moment. Time travel calls for maps, resources, and a common "Wally World or Bust" plan. Warren Buffet is famous for his folksy, insightful, and wordy shareholder letters. Look at the 79,743 words of the Google prospectus and consider the 64,000 words for the average novel. Google adds a few extra for their narrative. The first ten years of Google's story is a tale of culture and a magnetizing vision. Commenting on building an effective vision for the future, Dennis Berman in the *Wall Street Journal* called it a "$400 Billion Epistle."[28] On the other hand, consider brevity and Google's simple "Do no evil" mantra, a powerful "today and tomorrow" statement.

The ability to take others to a different place (travel) *and* time (vision) is a cardinal quality of leadership. Being the wizened sage on the mountaintop is not enough. Charisma calls for a collective—the synergy of fellow travelers. Today's fans join their respective tribe. These have names like Harley Owners Groups (HOGs), the Mickey Mouse Club, the Big Green Egg cooking group. To what tribes do you belong? How engaged are your customers?

Take a blank piece of paper and write what your purpose is going to be in the world for the next ten years. The inner conversation is insightful and stimulating. This exercise will help you focus on your vision. Charisma recruits with its leveraging and expanding quality. It naturally draws others and pulls out individual abilities with its magic. Fuel the fire of charisma with a flame that combines vision and time travel. With a clear vision of the future, you can leverage new resources. Like all fire, there needs to be something to ignite. That something will multiply your efforts—people.

A Parting Shot

The charismatic business draws in customers with their causes, and those future states that inspire. Charismatics gather others for a ride to "that" place. Communication is the vehicle. To be a great communicator to all involved will require you to hone your skills. What is your plan to get to the place of being a world class-presenter, to move people to a different future?

Chapter 8

Individual

Uniqueness Meets Abundance: Being 1,000% Better than the Competition

Great companies make meaning. A company has a name,
but its people give it meaning.
RICHARD PASCALE

Are Apple computer products charismatic? Their design takes in ease of use focus. Is it the product that is charismatic or the design that connects? Or is it something else? Add the iconic Steve Jobs and Apple technology develops a personality. People connect with personalities. Cultures are the religions of tribes or bands of employees; they create it and support it religiously.

The average and mundane business professes pushing relations down to the person who works directly with the customer. Then the average business fails to give organizational and financial resources. Like the brilliant flash of fireworks, the employee quickly learns the difference between lip service and real service.

Put your money where your mouth is. Disney gives the agents in their ticket booths the authority to spend up to $5000 to solve issues for their guests. Whether lost tickets, missing money, these cast members can instantly turn a disaster into a life-long memory of service and loyalty. Empowerment not given sends a message of "we don't trust you" from management.

You cannot be 100% better than your competition, but you can do 1,000 things 1% better if you enlist the skills of your stakeholders. Read that, employees. This requires a decentralization of decisions when it comes to addressing the needs of customers. The *Mohegan Sun* reinforced their mission of being considerate of the customer relationship by protecting the privacy of a lost guest.

"We just finished a training program for 7,500 employees called 'Every Guest, Every Time,'" says Don Trella, the executive in charge of team development at *Mohegan Sun*. "With all the competition, we must ensure that every guest interaction to not just be good enough. The customer interactions have to be great." Mohegan Sun knows their competition is not only other casinos located within driving distance, but also they must compete with Disney, Apple, and the other charismatic organizations.

These relationships are lowest level oriented. The CEO of a hospital cannot administer the healthcare needed by patients at 2:00 A.M. The president of Harley-Davidson cannot fix that leaky gasket on the iron horse in Kentucky. Personal relationships are just that—personal. They require real people who are valued for the work that only they can perform. The nurse, motor cycle mechanic, or security supervisor at the *Mohegan Sun* bring an individual contribution.

"Use your own best judgment at all times." This quote from Nordstrom's represents the entire content of the company's policy manual. When the individual employee contribution is empowered, then magical things occur.

Hire the best people, trust them, and then delegate with abandon.

FRANK VIZZARE

When each individual executes a 1% improvement, the competition does not stand a chance. To value the uniqueness of individuals is to leverage their contribution. This may well be the biggest difference between a manager and a leader. The manager sees individuals as a liability. The leader sees individuals as an asset. Remember the Gallup research that puts less than 30% of employees engaged? That is like taking out ten dollars, ripping up seven of them up.

The Chief Executive of the Year for *Chief Executive Magazine* in 2014 was Disney's Bob Iger. In the 2014 July/August issue, Iger was asked about his top priority when he took over as CEO. Said Iger:

> "While I had very specific and ultimately well-articulated strategic priorities for the company, first I wanted Disney to be admired and respected by the employees—cast members as we fondly call them—because if we ultimately were going to be admired and respected by our shareholders and by our customers, it had to start at home."[29]

IBM is one organization that found a place in our business charisma survey, albeit low on the standings. A dichotomy of the bland pin stripe suits and white shirts, the Big Blue culture has carried a mystique for decades. During his watch as Chairman and CEO of IBM, Thomas Watson Jr. summoned a young executive to his office. The young employee had made some bad decisions that cost IBM several million dollars.

"I suppose after that set of mistakes you will want to fire me," said the young associate.

"Not at all, young man, we have just spent a couple of million dollars educating you."[30]

Charismatic business knows power and influence are held by the employee, those individuals who fight the battle day in and day out. They are catered to, supported, encouraged, and respectfully engaged in dialogued.

> *The best leaders will be those who listen to their people to figure out where they should be going.*
>
> JACK KAHL

Charismatic business values the unique contributions of individuals much like Billy Beane did with the Oakland A's. The A's found success because of the unique abilities of undervalued players. Using the unique abilities of your business can make you powerful as well. Consider the Cubs.

In 1910, the Chicago Cubs possessed a legendary double-play trio. The play of Joe Tinker at shortstop, Johnny Evers at second base, and Frank Chance at first base had become a national catchphrase for predictability. The "Tinker to Evers to Chance" lexicon of expectedness became so powerful that it worked itself into poetic baseball speak. How many poems make it into the mainstream like Franklin Pierce Adams' words in the *New York Evening Mail*?

> "These are the saddest of possible words:
> 'Tinker to Evers to Chance.'
> Trio of bear cubs and fleeter than birds,
> 'Tinker and Evers and Chance.
> Ruthlessly pricking our gonfalon bubble,
> Making a Giant hit into a double —

Words that are heavy with nothing but trouble:
'Tinker to Evers to Chance.'"

To hit a groundball almost anywhere in the infield would subject the opponent to an almost certain Tinkers to Evers to Chance outcome. Celebrated and misunderstood. Why? They were great ball players, indeed expected to execute the double play. The fact was that Tinker and Evers could not stand each other. Off the ball field, they would walk in different directions to escape an encounter.

The real story was their teammate, Mordecai Peter Centennial "Three Fingers" Brown. Three Fingers ("Mort" to his friends) had suffered multiple injuries to his right hand. Missing his index finger from a farming accident and with broken fingers that were not set correctly, his misshapen hand allowed him to grip the baseball unlike any other human. The result was unnatural spin that made the ball squirrel and dance as it crossed the plate. Consequently, batters topped the ball only to hit grounders to Tinkers to Evers to Chance.

Is your organization looking at its unique employees and leveraging their insights, abilities, and talents? Is your HR department inflicting torture to ensure compliance? Are you a champion of seeing unique value in individuals? When organizations connect with the gifts of employees, there is a higher level of engagement as that DNS is infused throughout the business. Instead of seeing others as enemies and liabilities, you up the charisma factor when the mavericks, mavens, and misfits become trophies. Consider the charisma of the United States on the world's stage. The time-travel vision of Lady Liberty calls out to the diversity of individual contribution.

"Give me your tired, your poor,
Your huddled masses yearning to breathe free,

The wretched refuse of your teeming shore.
Send these, the homeless, tempest-tossed, to me:
I lift my lamp beside the golden door."

EMMA LAZARUS

What of the security guard who approaches little girls in their newly purchased princess dress, fresh off the rack at a Disney World gift shop? He approaches and says, "Excuse me, Princess, will you give me your autograph?" Aren't security guards

supposed to be big tough guys with security-encrusted devices on a leather belt? Are they really doing their job to make the day for a six-year-old Princess? Perhaps we should ask why all security guards are doing this?

Charismatic organizations capitalize on the individual. Apple has its Jonathan Ive, and Pixar has its John Lasseter. We have already written of the magic that Pixar mines with its Notes Day activity. These charismatic organizations search out these differences and reward their select employees. History tells us that men will work for less and even risk death if they believe they can contribute to a great cause.

My budget determined the ticket price of seating for a Las Vegas show. An usher took me down toward the side wing of the massive theater. "This is my first Cirque de Soleil performance," I said to the usher. "Hopefully I am close enough to see the performance well."

Five minutes before the show, my new usher friend touched my shoulder and quietly said, "Will you please follow me?"

Without fanfare, she moved me five rows from the stage in the center section of the theater.

OK! She had upgraded my seat to one whose value was three times the price I paid. And yes, the experience was all that and a trapeze to boot.

At the end of the performance I waited for the crowd to move out and approached the usher (research) to ask, "May I ask why you did that?"

Her answer had charisma all over it. It spoke of an organization who values the individual input of its employees. They also happen to be on the list of top charismatic organizations.

"Because of the lights our performers can't always see the audience," she said. "But we want them to see a full house where they can, so we try to fill in empty seats in the middle front." Do you move your customers into better seats so the employees feel more successful?

The country is full of good coaches. What it takes to win is a bunch of interested players.

DON CORYELL

If you have employees, you may have already lost. Perhaps you see them as a cost and a liability. Most do not contribute to the top line. They are often the most expensive part of a business. These living, breathing critters are the focus of other humans who see them as "resources" like you would see buildings, plants, and products. Human Resources managers often view them as ticking bombs, liabilities just waiting to go postal.

Janine Moon is an expert in career planning who works with companies that want to tap into the latent skills of their employees. She observed that "in most organizations you see the employees occupying space, but they are not engaged. They are corporate zombies." Her numbers are reflected in survey numbers by Gallup in their Q^{12} Meta-Analysis. Their research shows that only 13% of the workforce is "engaged." That means that 87% of the workforce are wandering around looking for a source plug for their umbilical. That is 9 out of 10 who are not engaged.

The measurables[31] for employees without engagement are profound:

- 31% more turnover without engagement (with some as high as 51%);
- 51% higher inventory "shrink"; and
- 62% more accidents.

The positive results for the engaged are equal in their impact:

- 27% less absenteeism;
- 12% higher customer satisfaction;
- 18% more productive; and
- 12% more profitable.

Charisma engages, its gravity pulling in employees and customers. When you have a critical mass of employees who are engaged, they have a time-travel vision, they have the tools, then the magic of charisma can start to work. To capture and leverage the ability of employees, you might have to stop seeing them as employees. Doctors who need to work on their bedside manners (charisma) *must* see nurses as an asset instead of suffering their relationship. Engineers will have to respect the insights of the lowly user of their expertise and take the feedback to improve and change their engineering.

A note to all managers: those direct reports hold the key to unlocking the innovation that should ooze from the pores of your department. Steve Jobs was a stickler for the simple, yet Apple created an elegant engineered product, and he knew he could expect it from his troops. He got it.

The world of charisma is not a pyramid with the leader at the top. "Remember your roots," said Jim Dixon, former CEO of CompuCom, as he poked the chest of a young executive (the author) some decades ago.

"Employees, hah!" exclaims the frustrated honcho. Charismatic businesses do not see them as just employees. In fact, they title them with by other titles: actors (Broadway), the crew (Trader Joe's), geniuses (Apple), and family (Zappos) or cast members (Disney).

I ask the Starbucks barista what her company calls her. She pipes cheerfully, "They call us 'partners.'"

When asked her take on "employees," one Starbucks district manager reacted with a grimace.

"I am sorry," she says. "It is just that that term is so foreign. These people are my partners in providing experiences for our customers." It sounds almost maudlin if it did not reflect so strongly in the charisma that Starbucks evokes.

If people relate to the company they work for, if they
form an emotional tie to it and buy into its
dream, they will pour their heart into making it better.

HOWARD SCHULTZ
CEO – STARBUCKS

A child that is loved has a thousand names. Theses partners, actors and the like *are* the business. The workers are the thoroughbreds, gifted "actors" whose job it is to facilitate performances for the paying customers. Changing what you call these individual workers is not all there is to it. That would be missing the point. It is more than a title. It is the fact that charisma comes from individuals who build the personal relationship with the customer. They create a culture, a personality that is the sum of the parts. Since honchos cannot be everywhere at once, they empower their troops with skills, talents, and tools to become the face, to be more exact, the *charismatic interface.*

This ability to empower individuals is seen in the phrase "Commander's Intent." Consider this excerpt from my book, *The Tips: The 7 Elements for Sales and Leadership that Drive High End Sales, Create Engaged Customers and Make the Competition Evaporate.*

> "In the military, a field general gives orders to his commanders, 'Take that hill!' He knows that when his people get into battle that the enemy is going to move their troops and resources. Great planning done many miles away will need some adaptations to succeed. Although those field officers may go left when their orders called for them to go right, they act with the commander's intent in mind. 'Take that hill!' is still the overall objective, even though they had to adapt in the moment to a different tactic.
>
> When your sales people are out there kicking down doors or creatively acting to get through the door in another way, it can be very easy for them to get sidetracked doing the wrong thing. It is imperative that they have commander's intent to keep them

focused. They need your hindsight, which creates foresight so that they get insight. They need a vision. They need a goal and direction—Commander's Intent."

Skills - Teaching the Craft of the Performance

The author was observing the three princesses: Cinderella, Snow White, and Sleeping Beauty, the live characters as they interacted with queued lines of little girls at Disneyland's Magic Kingdom. Each Disney Princess magically spoke to the star struck little girls in hushed tones. On cue, one of the little girls was turned 180° to face the waiting mommy-cam while the Princess cradled her little recruit within the folds of her beautiful gown. Immediately, you became aware of the training for these Disney characters. Each had been trained to hold their hands in a graceful princess form, like cradling an egg delicately within their fingers. The little girls smiled, but the character princesses smiles were *professional*.

"They don't blink," my wife mentions as we retreat.

"What?" I asked.

"The princesses don't blink when there is a possibility of a camera click."

Are you kidding? I watch for twenty minutes. Who trains their employees to not blink? One estimate puts a family Disney experience at close to $10,000 for a family of four for a week. You do not want to spend that kind of money, get home, and find out that Cinderella blinked during the big moment.

These customer interactions are about the stage production with your very own actors. Like the latest Broadway hit, there are rehearsals. Zappos requires a four-week training for every new employee, even new senior executives. This is training behavior to focus on the real target—the customer. Training provides skills, tools, and "how to tell the story." Practice creates mind-set and a performance. Hoping employees will just "get it" is for the average. Research shows that willpower is not enough to bring about change.[32] To send your employees through a day of customer service training is a "big business" knee jerk. Real change requires skills training that teach your people to "not blink."

Disney has a "college program" that recruits students for a summer intern stint at various Disney properties in an area that relates to their interest. "I was studying nursing," says one Business Charisma survey participant, "so I was asked if I would work as a lifeguard where medical training might be needed." On the first day, these students are immersed in the Disney Traditions course. They learn of the past, present and future of Disney in a class that is culture on steroids. The individual is always drenched with it when they join a charismatic cause. "Of course," says my participant, "we all lived in the Disney dorms and nobody had cars, so every night Disney provided transportation for us to go where we wanted. The whole thing was a fun and uplifting experience."

This is all about training management to value individuals. A skills training is essential to making individuals capable of providing for the customer. Sanctioning incompetence is common fare in the average organization. Stack rank any workforce staff and the bottom 20% represent the maximum allowed for bad performance. Those above that bottom 20% are thinking, "I may be bad, but if they are going to cut someone, then at least I am safe as long as the bottom feeders are around." The supervisors of this thinking must change their style.

When leaders allow the unique skills of their team to burst out, works of art are in the making. These skills are akin to the Stanislavskian methods used by the gifted Daniel Day-Lewis when he portrayed Abraham Lincoln in the Spielberg movie *Lincoln*. On and off the camera, Day-Lewis became so much a part of his presidential portrayal that even Steven Spielberg felt a need to wear a tie to work. Spielberg described making the movie *Lincoln* as an almost spiritual and sacred treatise. Do your employees see their work as sacred, spiritual? Is training new skills given this kind of importance?

Remember the opening of the Disney retail stores? The Disney University had to step up the training. The employees had to discover the average shopping experience, so they could learn what a shopping experience *should* look like.

I had an informal conversation with the manager of one Apple Computer Store in Mayfield, Ohio. "We often look for dyslexia in our job interviews. We find they do really well in our culture. They bring a unique perspective to our environment and see ways for our customers to improve their world. "We try to leverage the unique abilities of our employees to connect with our clientele. For example, sometimes we 'clap out' a customer when they make a big purchase."

"Clap out?" I ask with raised eyebrows.

"Yes, we want the customer to feel good and our own team members to be involved in the business. As the customer is heading out the door with their bagged product, one of the staff will start applause—more of a Congratulations! Other team members join in, and before the customer gets out of the door, even other customers are clapping. It sounds weird, but it can be very cool." Here's building a personal relationship one customer at a time.

The order-taking "partner" at a Starbucks is trained to ask for the customer's name and where they put that name on the coffee cup. Friends know each other's name. Did Coca-Cola steal the insight with their popular "Friends" campaign and "buy your friend a Coke"?

At a Disney theme park, one of the most important jobs belongs to the Street Sweepers. These white uniformed worker-bees have been a major focus for Disney. They receive special training because experience shows they are asked so many questions. "Can you tell me where the rest rooms are?" and "Will you take our picture?" requests are common—all of that while keeping the park spotless.

In addition to sweeping, some of them started using their brooms as paintbrushes. They put some water in their dustpans, dip in the broom's bristles, and create Disney characters on the pavement. Of course, the water paintings only last for a few minutes, but the guests are enthralled. How much personality can a janitor have? Once Disney discovered these unique talents, they brought in real cartoon artists and trained the sweepers in the finer nuances of drawing Mickey. Do not fight those employees who have something out of the norm. Encourage it. Revel in it.

Starbucks decided to ask partners (employees) about ways to provide a better customer experience. Steaming milk changes the flavor if it sits too long. The "spilled" milk that had to be poured down the drain affected profits. One employee asked, "Why not put marks on the inside of the steamer cups, then steam enough to service those who are in line?" The ridiculously simple observation has saved tens of millions of dollars.

Capture the unique abilities of your people and use those abilities to deliver charisma. It is easy when the talent of your worker is like Idina Menzel playing *Elphaba*. Finding the latent abilities of your workers requires a stop to "grass is greener" thinking. "If I just had employees like old XYZ down the street, then we could really do something." This excuse is really a co-dependency statement by managers who are in need of creativity and innovation training.

Can an executive who is named Writz Carlton not be charismatic? Randolph "Randy" Carlton Writz is a senior executive of one of the country's most successful chain of Wendy's hamburger franchises. With laser intensity he encourages their employees to give "customer wow and beyond," encouraging them to listen to the customer and then brainstorm unique solutions. He shared," one thing that I have learned and helped with our success is that you can not over appreciate your people or your customers. We give dog treats at our carry out windows and go around with mints in the dining room thanking customers for eating with us. I have never had an employee tell me I thanked them to much or complemented them to much. Happy employees make happy customers. "There is the classic scene in the movie *Money Ball* when the team manager, played by the late Philip Seymour-Hoffman, refused to put in the players that Billy Beane gives him. Beane, played by Brad Pitt, trades the vaunted player away, forcing the coach to play his pick. It is a great lesson in dancing with those you came with. If the child cannot see or understand the new skill, is it the fault of the student or the teacher? In the case of Billy Ball and the Oakland A's, the new math skills of recruiting quirky players and playing to their strengths make for a great movie and a winning team. Safe!

While my brother was staying at a hotel, he asked for directions to a local jewelry store. The desk manager asked what he was looking for. His watch battery had just died, my brother explained. The manager wondered if he might leave his watch for an hour so he, the manager, could do some research. On his way out for dinner, the manager called him over to give him back his watch with a new battery installed! He was informed, "It is no problem, and one of our guys got you a new battery. No charge."

Who does this sort of thing? (Note: this hotel sent out people to scrape the windows of snow and ice on the cars in their parking lot the next morning. Who does this stuff?) To get customer wow takes individuals. It is easy for the leader to preach the need for "customer wow." To get wow and beyond—to plant and grow charisma—takes people who entertain and service with class. If the organization does not have resources dedicated to building these skills in their employees, then most likely the magic of charisma will flutter just out of reach.

Just north of Akron, Ohio, is a small grocery story, the West Point Market. Charismatic to their clientele, this store specializes in all the standard food products, but each possesses a slight twist. When Sally Hogshead indicates that customers will pay up to 50% more for fascinating offerings, I think she has the West Point Market in mind. Shopping there will not get you the best prices. West Point is mesmerizing and charismatic though.

I stand in front of their expansive deli counter with Tom Loraditch, the store's Executive Chef. How many grocery stores do you know that have a chef on the staff? He explains that once a week the executive team gathers in a meeting where new items are considered.

"A while ago, one of our employees brought a salad, a relish of sorts, to the meeting. It was dark, almost black in color. With suspicion, each sampled the dish. Approvals from all put the new dish into the family of fantastic deli offerings. When someone asked what it should be called, one participant quipped, "Well, it sure is ugly."

"Let's call it Ugly Salad then," the others offered.

What daring soul who has come to trust their local charismatic business would not want to sample some Ugly Salad? Do you have to teach innovation and creativity to employees? It helps. When the eclectic is valued and encouraged, fun erupts.

Nancy is just your typical Southwest Airlines flight attendant. She shared how she took the plastic dry cleaning bag out of the closet in her hotel room, cut it open so it was a large "canvas," and made an impromptu poster proclaiming "Happy Birthday!" She and her cohort-in-crime flight attendant hung the poster across the hotel door of their traveling fellow worker, the First Mate. He opens his door only to run into a door wide sign celebrating his birthday so far away from family. Cost to the Southwest? Zero. Value to the flight attendants and the pilot? Invaluable. This stuff bleeds into the customer interaction.

Charismatic Organizations Play

In the early morning hours before the Disney park opens, an annual contest occurs. Teams of cast members race around Tom Sawyer's Island in a contest of large canoes powered by teams. With competition as fierce as any NFL playoff game, the team members, dripping in sweat, give high-fives and cheers as they qualify for moving upward in their bracket. Even their names speak of the culture and fun of the event:

- Haulin' Oars
- Canoe and Improved
- Paddlin' Bayou
- Last of the Rowhicans
- Paddle your Behind
- Canoe Kids on the Block

Are you employees playing? Are there regular celebrations? Are your individuals rewarded for personal interactions? Nordstrom's rewards the employee of the month with plaques and additional employee discounts. How to win? Get the most unsolicited comments and satisfaction letters from customers.

They Are Talking . . . but Are You Listening?

One of the biggest reasons people leave their employer is either because of a boss who is a pill or a supervisor who just does not care about the individual. A person can look like they are listening and yet not hear a word. Authentic listening (interest) brings gratitude, which is the building block for personal warmth and presence. This personal warmth is the foundation of charisma.

Interest>gratitude>personal presence>charisma

The boss who has a sense of humor is three times more likely to succeed. Although I fly often, the most memorable was a Southwest flight with a Cracker Jack flight attendant who made a two hour flight non-stop fun. Fun is Five Guys Hamburgers who pitch their logo T-Shirts with the caveat, "customized catsup and mustard stains applied by the customer." It is worth it to call Zappos customer service just to hear the corny joke of the day.

Charisma comes when leaders use self-deprecating humor. Charisma comes with good-hearted banter between workers and customers. This is not the sarcastic, mean-spirited humor of autocrat managers gone wild. The humor of charisma comes in finding the absurdity of the common, and even—Heaven forbid!—taking things too seriously.

When stakeholders take themselves too serious, they suck the whole culture down the dark hole of the self-absorbed. If the leaders in the organization are pickle suckers, then they train their employees to seek out the pickle barrel. When a team member with a "bad attitude" enters the charismatic organization, they often self-select themselves off the team. This usually occurs before they are "de-hired." Charisma is seldom found where entitlement, tenure, or unions protect the self-serving inward focus. Research tells us that kids do better academically when they sleep later into the morning. Many schools have mandated early start times because the focus is on schedules of others who are not the students. Is it really that alarming that online education is gaining such momentum?

Gold Stars

What child is not excited to go home and show their parent their gold star? Has the world treated us so poorly that we cannot give out gold stars to adults? "I didn't get any, so I am not giving any," says the inward focused supervisor. Come on.

Charisma celebrates—a lot. Charismatic organizations search high and low for ways to motivate their workers. Any behavior that should be emulated should be acknowledged and rewarded.

> *You call these baubles . . . well; it is with baubles that men are led. Do you think that you would be able to make men fight by reasoning? Never. That is good only for the scholar in his study. The soldier needs glory, distinctions, rewards.*

NAPOLEON

Marshall Dahneke, President of Hygenic, a charismatic company that manufactures surgical latex and related products in the Akron, Ohio area, is the kind of leader who understands the power in individuals. Months after we did a strategic planning session he asked me, "What do I do after Snickers?"

"Snickers?" I ask.

"You suggested I find my executive team doing good things and then reward them with a Snickers bar at the next meeting. You know something that is quick and inexpensive. The problem is that no one is eating his or her Snickers bars. They have them lined up on top of their filing cabinets as a kind of trophy case."

Is it the value of the reward or the magic of recognition? Ask a mother of adult children if she would do it differently now that her kids are grown. The candid answer is always, "I wish I had paid more attention to my darlings." What is your focus on the care and feeding of your "darlings"? What are your customer interaction initiatives? How are you rewarding those who most emulate great performances with the client?

Some years ago, I fought my own cancer battle. The hospital probably could be considered charismatic based on many of the MAGNETIC qualities. As I trekked to the daily treatments, I got to know Denise and Leslie. These two ladies were at the front desk for the oncology department and were the face of the institution day after day. One day I stopped to get a sucker out of a small candy bowl that perched on their receptionist desk. After Denise came out from giving a treatment, she reached up and set the candy bowl down by her phone. I thought, *I didn't ask earlier. I wonder if I did something wrong?*

The next day I asked, "Does the hospital buy the candy or do you two fund the sweets?" They then told me that some of their cancer patients have a strong metal taste in their mouth after their procedure. Out of their own pockets they buy candy for their patients. Are your employees so dedicated to your cause that they donate their own time and money to grow your business?

You cannot play the game if you do not wear the uniform. I once interviewed an explosives engineer. I asked him, "Do you tell your employees, 'Now don't drop this box of dynamite'"?

"No, but we do tell them to be careful." The former gets them thinking about dropping the box. Setting the stage, coaching the interaction is essential, especially when the employee is handling explosives. The right uniforms and costumes are a necessity. The right tools and arena are a given.

While I sat next to Chad Hoopes in a meeting, I watched him pull out a plastic egg, pop it open and remove a large glob of Silly Putty. For the next twenty minutes he discreetly massaged the mass in his fingers. At the end of the meeting, I asked him what he was doing.

"To have the strength in your smaller fingers to hold the strings to the neck of the violin is key to classic sound. I use the Silly Putty to build that strength."

Chad is a winner of the Yehudi Menuhin International Violin Competition. When you hear him give voice to his instrument with orchestras and symphony groups worldwide, you understand the value of Silly Putty. If Charisma is a divine gift that influences others, Chad can bring tears to your eyes with his gift of charisma both in his music and in him as an individual.

What Silly Putty tools do your employees need? Disney University stages an after-hours trivia scavenger hunt for cast members. With the purpose of arming their employees with knowledge of the product (the theme park) they bungee-cord together teams and give them a list of quests. Each quest educates, informs, and builds the working knowledge of their product with the various trivia clues.

When the custodial staff mistakenly cleaned the haunted mansion just prior to the opening of Disney Japan, a group of experts in cobwebs and dust had to be flown again across the Pacific to "haunt" the mansion again. One employee may think a lack of cobwebs is clean, but the customer wants them. Whether it is Silly Putty or cobwebs, what tools do your employees need?

Trader Joe's has their top secret "Crew Member Passport," a pocket-sized instruction manual that addresses the store's bell system, tour of the bathrooms, and a whole chapter on "Wow Customer Experiences." They see their demo kiosk as a place of "infotainment."

On the Disney Jungle Cruise, the ship commanders have "spieled" for fifty years. Constantly changing, the humorous banter is fixed, improved, and updated. Adlibbing is allowed a little, but the guarantee of funny comes from the tool of the script. Kids still ride it because of the robotic animals. To the child those critters still have the suspense of real tigers, elephants, and hippos. The adults are along for the shtick.

> "Ladies and gentlemen, your attention please. Would the party that lost the roll of fifty $20 bills wrapped in a red rubber band please report to the turnstile? We have good news for you. We found your red rubber band."

> "Let me get one thing straight. If we start to sink, the captain will be going down with the boat. I would like you to meet your new captain (look at nearby guest). What did you say your name was?"

Do you value the individuals in your organization? Are you a natural Undercover Boss, instilling a burning desire to give them the tools to get the job done? Do they leverage their individual strengths to lift the performance of others? Are the employees who are funny sharing their "spiel" with others so all can be seen as humorous, caring, and serving? Do they have the Silly Putty necessary to become the best in the world? Business charisma is 1,000 fellow travelers, each doing something 1% better. That is the dream of your customer and the nightmare of the competition.

A Parting Shot

Training is not a one time thing. Every true professional has
a coach, trainer, or consultant. Sharpen the Saw is a basic
building block for every leader. If you do not have a regular,
impactful training program for your employees, then charisma
will ever float out of reach. How do skills develop without
practice? You will want to raise the level of the customer
relationship and then train others how to make that happen.
You will need to teach skills just to deal with the concepts in
the next chapter. That alone will make you stand out.

Chapter 9

Charity

The End Game . . . Significance above Success.

Caring is the ultimate competitive advantage.
RON KENDRICK

We do not attain the victory of life by selfishness.
Victory is for those who give themselves to causes
beyond themselves. It is very biblical and very true
that everyone who exalts themselves will be humbled,
and he who humbles himself will be exalted.
(FORMER SENATOR JOHN DANFORTH
at the funeral of Katharine Graham,
Former Chair of the Board of *The Washington Post*)

Though I speak with the tongues of men and of angels, and
have not charity, I am become as
sounding brass or a tinkling cymbal.
1 CORINTHIANS 13:1

Tom Peters, the storied business consultant, was pacing the stage at the end of another of his thousands of engagements. This presentation was in Salt Lake City before a packed house.

Having poured decades of insights and wisdom onto the gathered executives, he paused before his last few comments. Hands in pockets, blazer over a V-neck sweater, shoes appropriately scuffed like a professor, his chin down, he strides the width of the stage looking at the floor.

At stage edge he stops, looks up and says, "I guess what it is all about . . . ." His voice trails off for emphasis. ". . . is that you really have to love people. If you do not, please go do something else. Everything else just doesn't matter as much as truly caring about people."

Business charisma has at its keystone this love, this caring for others. *Love* tends to be a warm and fuzzy type of word to business people. Let us instead use a more mature word: *charity*. We often associate charity with the gift to the homeless person. Instead, think of the caring and attention you give to another. Isn't that a gift of sorts? Think of providing a service or product that lifts the life of the customer in a way they cannot do themselves. Isn't that a gift?

Creativity may come and go. Execution ebbs and flows. The narrative and stories may or may not connect. The "stage play" may not resonate with the customer. Charity is the constant in charisma. It is the mainstay and heart. It never fails, says Paul. It is sincere. The word "sincere" comes from a practice of faking out the buyer of a marble statue by filling in the mistakes with marble dust and a wax paste that fills the error. Sin = without - cere = wax. No excuses. No hiding behind some policy or "that's it . . . that is what they have given us to work with. Sorry."

The conference was about to start, with me being the opening keynote speaker. One last check of my Power Point slides revealed that the laptop power supply had died. I took the hotel shuttle to the nearby Apple Computer Store. My Apple Genius confirmed the death of the power supply and revealed that the expiration of the warranty on the part had lapsed by less than sixty days. What would they do? They had a unique part that was not available anywhere else, and time was of the essence. They had the authority *and* the power (more puns), the command and the clout to extract whatever the cost. These low-level Apple employees leaned on me (at my request for the photo). "Why don't we just make you whole? You have a presentation to make, and we think we can cover you."

The single most powerful element of business charisma is charity found in the good will toward the customer (or employee) by those who have the good will to give. When the lowly customer is at your mercy, then you have a unique opportunity to use warmth and service to meet their needs. It is like a parent who controls life sustenance so you can control value for the customer. When there is an act of charity for those who may not be able to give back, then meaningful relationships blossom. Charisma is given by the customer when they *feel* their best interest is the intention.

In charismatic organizations, there is an acute awareness of delivering this warmth and presence. It starts at the top and permeates the whole. The focus is on what the recipient *feels,* and they do remember the feeling of warmth, personality, charm, and caring—charisma.

The one piece of advice which will contribute more to making you a better leader, will provide you with greater happiness and self-esteem and at the same time advance your career more than any other advice, and it doesn't call for a special personality, and it doesn't call for any certain chemistry . . . and anyone can do it, and the advice is that you must care.

LT. GENERAL MELVIN ZAIS

To those who are empowered with the ability to be charitable to customers, fellow employees, or to everyone in general, the benefits are powerful. At the Center for Investigating Healthy Minds at the Waisman Center of the University of Wisconsin at Madison, research points to benefits for those who are compassionate. Researchers found that those who were taught compassion skills displayed increased brain activity in the regions associated with empathy and understanding. It would seem that a focus on customers as "guests" (Disney) and service to them only increases the physical (brain elasticity) ability to perform that service at a higher level.

Brain scans show that "acts of kindness" registered more like eating chocolate than fulfilling an obligation. "The same pleasure centers light up when we receive a gift as when we donated to charity," reports ABC's Dan Harris.[33]

Harris goes on to say, "Overall, compassionate people tended to be healthier, happier, more popular, and more successful at work."

Even Darwin gets into the act. In his work *Humans,* he observed, "A tribe, including many members who, from possessing in a high degree the spirit of patriotism, fidelity, obedience, courage, and sympathy, were always ready to aid one another and to sacrifice themselves for the common good and would be victorious over most other tribes." Moral: Be fit and be nice. Charity wins.

"We hire for personality because we can teach the technical part of the business," says one Starbucks manager. She shared that the ability to connect, to listen empathetically to others is essential. "I need a more homespun partner (employee) than the store two miles away. They are more business oriented, whereas we cater to the neighborhood-oriented customer. So I sometimes recommend certain job applicants to go visit my sister store."

When I work with various leadership groups I draw the following diagram. "What do you think of the four areas?" I ask the audience. The answers always come back the same.

In the upper right hand corner are those technically competent workers who are great at connecting with the customer. They know how to make a Starbucks cup of coffee and have a conversation at the same time.

To the top left are those personalities who are still learning the technical aspects. These people have the capability to connect with others. Feed them oxygen, and encourage them upward to become a star. At the bottom left are those employees who are neither people oriented or have any technical skills. When asked what they would title this group, workshop

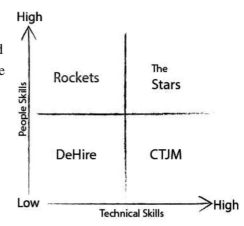

attendees used such words as losers, "need to be working elsewhere," "speed bumps," or the classic "dehire."

At the bottom right is an especially prickly group. These people are very competent at their tradecraft, but they do not always connect well with people. If it includes those who work alone, say programmers, their technical skills warrant a solitary effort. In charismatic organizations, these people most often need to have a CTJM (Come to Jesus Meeting). (Note: political correctness aside, this term is the most appropriate for this group. If it offends, please forgive.)

To a person in this CTJM group, a private conversation should occur that sounds like, "Listen, you are very good at what you do, but that is not enough. We need you to step up your people skills." Have them read this book. They must realize that customers (or fellow workers) will go where they can get a good emotional relationship. They must understand higher profits, better employee morale, and a host of other benefits that are objectives, and that these benefits come from charisma. Should the CTJM people rationalize "that is not my job," then the meeting is not over. For someone in the CTJM quadrant the message "unacceptable" must clearly be communicated. No threats are necessary (at least initially). Just give a calm, clear message of the imperative to move beyond customer satisfaction, past awesome customer experiences and all the way to customer engagement. Charisma is the goal. People skills are an absolute, and the CTJM must start developing and using them like a man on a sinking ship who does not know how to swim. He must learn swimming skills now . . . or else.

> *Leadership is solving problems. The day soldiers stop bringing you their problems is the day you have stopped leading them. They have either lost confidence that you can help or concluded you do not care. Either case is a failure of leadership.*
>
> COLIN POWELL

Charisma is all about listening. Eighty percent of charisma is given by the other person, that is, the customer, when they feel heard and understood. "But our policy is . . ." is the antithesis to charisma. Customer service training is a commodity. It is the ante for the game. It is, however, far from the emotional relationship of charismatic organizations that move to a higher level than just providing service.

For example, consider the simple question of a flight attendant. The passenger is asked what they would like to drink. "Pepsi," comes the reply. The flight attendant says, "I am sorry, but we don't carry Pepsi products (create an emotional engagement). Would a Coke possibly work?" The customer is asked to sacrifice. If the flight attendant fails to say, "I am sorry but . . . " then a connection of the heart is missed.

Businesses that are on the prowl for ways to needle the next dollar out of their customers will never attain charisma. The last thing those businesses want is to be charitable. Instead of approaching business with a philosophy of abundance, theirs is "how do we get every part of the pie we can get without ticking off the customer?" Call it revenue by a thousand cuts.

Consider the cable and cell phone companies whose monthly rates drop for new customers, but when the existing customer discovers they have been overpaying, they don't apologize but capitulate and lower the fees to the loyal (read as sucker) customer. Following suit is the airlines that charges for luggage and then charges extra to get on the plane early so you can put the luggage you would have checked into the overhead bins before the space runs out. Cut, cut, cut. Bleed, bleed, bleed.

One giant Las Vegas property has steps leading up the monorail that ferries visitors up and down the Strip. The steps are only forty-seven footsteps from the front door. Instead, this property makes you walk for a half-mile past their shops to get to the monorail. Buy more in our shops, gamble more, and to heck with what you the customer wants. Sacrifice.

How many hours do patients sit waiting for the doctor? Much of the healthcare world is moving to compensation that keys on patient satisfaction. Yes, an unhealthy bedside manner will hit the doctor's wallets. Lack of bedside manners will eventually result in higher costs and fewer customers. Like the Starbucks manager, medical schools are learning that being smart is not enough. The astute clinician doctor who ticks off the patient will eventually reap the higher malpractice costs.[34] Doctors that are liked tend to get sued less. The technically competent doctor may well have higher costs than the physician with great bedside manners.

When you ask the customer to sacrifice, a line is crossed, and the emotional "bank account balance" had better be there to offset the lower value of the relationship. The charismatic business knows that the customer wants what they want, and to not give up value because the business needs to squeeze additional revenues from somewhere. Charity and charisma are never found looking inward. When someone defines love by looking inwardly, they can never move to charisma. Charisma gives, serves, and focuses on the other person—the customer. The warmth and magic comes from giving as much as possible.

From Ed Staros of the group that developed the Ritz-Carlton Hotel Company we read: "I remember in the late eighties there were economic concerns, and [with] other hotels doing things like cutting out mouthwash and changing the flower arrangements. Horst Schultz was adamant always that we were not going to cut costs and maintain any lasting success. Just because the economy was bad, it did not mean the guest didn't want mouthwash. Rather than cutting back, we wanted to be more efficient and even improve our product . . . . If you're a widget factory and there are twenty steps to make a widget, and you study your business with a systematic approach to improving quality and you figure out you can make an improved widget in eighteen steps, all the better. Essentially, that was our quest: to not cut corners but to become more focused and to get the maximum quality . . . ."[35]

To create the emotion-based customer experiences that are at the core of charisma requires a look at the cardinal qualities involved in the charitable actions for the client. Charity then is a gift. When you give a gift and then look for something in return, charisma will not flow. Charismatic leaders are known for their selflessness. Their self-sacrifice is inspiring to others.

Many years ago, the movie titled *The Magnificent Obsession,* starring Jane Wyman and Rock Hudson, had a plot of an alcoholic playboy whose selfish and spoiled actions took the life of a local hero. Driven to understand the life of the victim who is lost due to his own self-interest, Bob Merrick (Hudson) discovers a life of giving, love, and charity that then changes his life and others around him. The magnificent obsession comes from giving without expectation of receiving. Too often businesses use the Godfather dogma of "someday I will come and ask a favor in return of you." True loyalty (of customers) comes from the moral obligation of returning in kind because it is the right thing to do, not because someone is compelled. In the case of the Mafia, loyalty is really twisted into fear and dread, which are not qualities of charity and hence not charismatic for a business.

To get business charisma is to be charitable toward customers. Charity, with its presence and warmth grows out of gratitude. Unless you truly appreciate the customer deeply and authentically then gratitude will not flow. The previous chapter addresses the need to focus on the unique and different contributions of your own employees and stakeholders. Charisma looks at the customer's challenges. Where they are going? How are they going to get there? It is about asking questions. When you truly "see" their world clearly, you will also see opportunities. It is the difference between presenting *from* and being present *with.*

One family went to Disney with their little daughters who brought with them their stuffed teddy bears. When they went off to one of the parks, the parents instructed the girls to leave their teddy bears in the room. When they returned at the end of the day, they found the bears sitting at the table with a tea party spread in front of them. The next day the Disney hotel put the bears in front of the TV with some snacks. Some Disney cast member saw a little girl's teddy bear and thought of a loving and playful gift that only they could give. The emotion and joy of that charitable service is the stuff of legends. It is what makes someone want to take his or her vacation *with* the charismatic.

Charisma > Charity > Listen profoundly > Gratitude > Loyalty is assigned

Apple Computer under Steve Jobs had this charisma. He knew what was cool due in part to his focus on design as a value. He translated technology that others invented into something that touched the heart of his customers. He picked up an iPad prototype and observed that it had an edge that didn't feel warm and connecting. It felt boxy. Charisma is thinking, "I want it to feel warm and personable."

Being Much More

You used to be much more...muchier. You've lost your muchness.

LEWIS CARROLL
Alice in Wonderland

To become magnetic will test your courage. Start with baby steps and you will quickly find yourself standing out. You can become more, so much more, to your customers.

Starbucks' keystone leader, Howard Schultz, found himself re-reading Pine and Gilmore's *Experience Economy* book. He then started backing up on some of the store practices so the customer could feel the full coffee experience of fresh grinding and brewing. It would have been very businesslike to cut costs and grind, bag and ship coffee from a centralized facility. Lower costs mean higher profits.

Really? "I don't know why I continue to go to Starbucks even though I know the coffee costs twice as much," says one respondent in our Charisma Survey. "I guess I just like the smell and the feel." At Chick-Fil-A the phrase "It would be my pleasure" is the response to any customer who says "Thank you." Provide the service, get the customer's thanks, and then one-up the relationship with a heartfelt "It would be my pleasure." In several surveys, the respondents said they frequent Chick-Fil-A just because they love the politeness and courtesy.

Charisma is the Blue Door Café in Cuyahoga Falls, Ohio. It is the theatrics of buying pecan rolls from the glass case before they are gone. The menu proclaims fresh ingredients in terms that rival a Victoria's Secret fashion show. Their menus read like a book, a veritable J. Peterman catalogue.

Charisma is Victoria's Secret, where you pay more for less. It is the emotion VS creates in the imagination of a future event. Victoria's Secret is all about time-travel. Charisma is the Disney experience for the biggest show on earth. Who cares that the streets are steam cleaned at night? Who cares that hundreds of thousands of light bulbs are changed each week at the Disney properties? Who cares that one of the largest navies in the world is found at Disney theme parks? Who teaches princesses to not blink when their character is photographed with a guest? Should not all street sweepers be given training to draw cartoons on concrete sidewalks with their brooms? Who pays attention to the fact that people don't "walk"? Disney knows their guests saunter. You won't find

90° turns on Disney sidewalks. It takes several smaller angles to get around a corner. Who pays this kind of attention to the customer?

Charisma is Zappos, where one legendary customer service call was clocked at eight hours in length. One call. When others hear that statistic, they often ask, "What do you talk about for eight hours on one call?" Charisma comes from listening. Eight hours of dialogue is the stuff of legends.

This brings us back to the beginning. How many classes (math class, meetings, and training sessions) did you successfully navigate during your life? Hundreds? How many teachers (leaders, business people) have been significant in *your* world? Your compass points to these people. They moved past success and created significance. They were charismatic.

You have the choice to stay on the path that leads to an emotional engagement. You have the choice of focusing on the internal business needs or discovering how much brighter the noonday sun will become when you look to building a relationship with customers. When you give charisma, there is a whole new world above the clouds. Every human interaction becomes a feast of joy, of lifting, of putting a dent in the universe. Come to the bright side of the force—the force of charisma.

Chapter 10

Personal Charisma

"Lack of charisma can be fatal."
JENNY HOLZER

"Let the others have the beauty. I've got the charisma."
CARIE ROITFELD

When you ask a question of a person who is charismatic, their look is always the same. They have the "it" factor, a magical warmth and presence that creates an aura that is catnip to others. Their response to the simple, "Do you consider yourself charismatic?" always looks the same. Their smile is slight, with nuances of humility. They have an overall look that is a little perplexed. They know they have "it" but don't always understand how they got it. Modern research, however, is discovering what behaviors and habits make these unique people so magical. We know now what they do, either consciously or unbeknownst to them, to make them magnetic to others.

Mitch has "it"—character. Bigger than life, he is kind of person who wears his clothes out from the inside, a constant blur of energy and activity. He seems to be bouncing instead of walking. When he turns his attention to you, you become the only person in the room.

His name is Mitch Burton. He started his career as a bricklayer. After many years he was at the top of a construction company he created. He was voted the number one luxury homebuilder in the competitive San Diego market. He then took his wealth and moved into other pursuits. He, like a lot of charismatic people, has his ardent fans, and then there are those who totally just don't see "it." Like most who have personal charisma, they can turn it on and off at will.

Another charismatic is Mike Talentino. He might not be the biggest personality in the room, but when you walk away from a conversation, you feel like someone *finally* listened to you, just you. No judgments. The conversation easily saunters around what is going on in your world with clarifying questions, each driving home the unspoken point that you are the center of attention. You feel that what you are doing, thinking, or feeling counts.

Mike is not an extrovert. He is, however, the kind of acquaintance that you wish you were around more. Months after a conversation, he will call or connect via social media with a "How are you doing?" He too has a gift to make you feel like you are the only person in the room. Do you feel like he has ulterior motives, some hidden agenda? Never. You feel safe, trust, and comfort.

> *A friend is one to whom one may pour out the contents of one's heart, chaff and grain together, knowing that gentle hands will take and sift it, keep what is worth keeping, and with a breath of kindness, blow the rest away.*
>
> GEORGE ELIOT

Is it a gift? On the other hand, is it a set of skills? If you were looking for description on how to describe Mike, the word charismatic would probably not come to mind. He exudes warmth and asks questions that make your mind share the present and easily move to the future. "So what are you going to do?" might come a heartfelt inquiry.

Mike is the everyday kind who has that special something that is charisma. He makes you feel like you matter. I am sure he has an off-day occasionally. Aside from that, he has serious skills to listen. He is just like a charismatic business and has a similar magnetism:

- Cares about you (a **m**ission to provide extreme, severe service);
- Is interested in your world (the **a**rena . . . or stage of your life);
- Connects with your values (the trust created by **g**ravitas);
- Wants to know what is happening in your world (**n**arrative of your stories);
- Compliments and supports your unique abilities (your **e**clectic or unnatural behavior);
- Encourages your future plans (**t**ime travel);
- Their focus is on you. Here, now, in the present (**i**ndividuals and their contribution); and
- Listens with warmth and presence (**c**harity).

That is what a charismatic person will do for you. How they do this has some common building blocks:

- Self-sacrificing;
- They look the part;
- They provide service to others or to a greater cause;
- Are ethical;
- Focus on change as necessary to alter the status quo;
- Vision (future oriented);
- Great listeners; and
- Great communicators.

The list could go on. You could find plenty of titles addressing these qualities. Consider "The 22½ Principles of Leadership" or "The 3 Big Secrets of Leaders." (Don't look for these. I made them up.) We are not talking about leadership (although one study indicates that charisma makes a leader twice as effective). We are talking about you. How do you get more charisma? This book is not about creating a vision or ethics. It is about making you (or your business) more charismatic. If *you* are the business, then why not make your product more magnetic, charismatic and mesmerizing?

We know that charismatic people:

- Get better performance reviews;
- Are rewarded with more raises in pay;
- Are more likely to be promoted;
- Are happier;
- Others listen to what they say more readily;
- Make a bigger impression;
- They are more likely to get along with fellow workers; and
- They sell more.

The list goes on, but you get the idea. If you breathe in air, then you will benefit from developing your charisma skills.

Are extraverts more charismatic than introverts? Just like businesses, a person does not have to be outgoing to be charismatic. Al Williams is another charismatic character from my past who was a partner in crime in rolling out no-name generics to the retail grocery stores in the late 1970s. Once he chided me to "stay quiet" about what we were doing. "You will want to brag and show off, but we do not want others to know about what we are doing until *after* we have stolen the market from them." So, for personal and business charisma, is it better to be an introvert or an extrovert? It really doesn't matter because the customer is the one who assigns charisma, the one who determines who has this magical *je ne sais quoi*. Since 80% of charisma is assigned to people who listen well, it doesn't really matter if the listener is outgoing or more inward oriented.

In fact, there are a lot of loud, outgoing, obnoxious extraverts who will never be charismatic because they are too busy being full of themselves to stop and pay attention to others. I often do training to teach sales people how to say less and sell more. We give them physical tools that force them to listen better.

What is essential for personal charisma is the ability to listen with advanced skills. Think of Apple computer and the two "Steve's." The extraverted Steve Jobs (although some would say he was an introvert) was a complimentary foil match to the introvert Steve Wozniak.

A note about time: research indicates that we mentally live 95% of the time in the past or the future. We replay past events or worry and feed the boogie monsters who might materialize and obliterate us with their ray guns. To really harness personal charisma requires you to be in the here-and-now. That 5% of your mental work will need to expand.

It is estimated that we speak at 200 to 400 words per minute (with the author hitting speeds of 500 wpm at times). Meanwhile the listener is thinking at about 3,000 words—ten times faster. So what does the listener do mentally? The listener drifts into the future and past in their mind. Their head is nodding just as if any good listener would be doing. Meanwhile, the listener is going over their to-do list or mentally planning the coming weekend. They might be wondering why the person talking doesn't do something about their bad breath.

Just as others can see a fake smile, they also have the ability to see if you are listening with 100% of your attention. We are very good at sensing this and often increase the emotion of our words to get the listener back to listening. When the person talking senses you listening with 100% of your mind, a magic occurs. Charisma gets legs. If you the listener can control the 95% of your mental time and be *in the present,* then the other person will describe you as someone who "made me feel like I was the only person in the room."

Being present is a behavior—a skill that can and will grow with practice. Personal charisma is gained by developing skills that will help you connect with others in deeper ways.

Charisma Skills

Years ago Marilyn Monroe was with a photographer and the editor of *Redbook*. The group was walking on a street in New York City. Monroe turned and asked the group, "Shall I be her?" In a moment, she fluffed her hair and stuck a pose there on the sidewalk. Immediately someone called out "Marilyn Monroe!" In moments a crowd gathered, with people shoving and pushing to get a glimpse of the star. With a great deal of effort, she was extricated away from the press of the public.[36] Norma Jean Mortenson showed her learned ability to become charismatic. On command she could become Marilyn Monroe. She had skills that could be turned on at will.

Those who are described as charismatic don't always know the "when, where or how" of their learning to being magnetic. If you press them a little, you will get a wry smile and acknowledgement of having "it." Somewhere, somehow, they learned the skills just as a piano player learns their craft by practicing each note repeatedly. With feedback or positive results in dealing with others, they became charismatic.

Amp up your personality with warmth and presence. In the following pages we will look at skills that, with practice, can become as much of who you are as tying your shoes or writing your name.

Four levels of learning occur as you develop new skills. Developed by Noel Burch of Gordon Training International group, the Four Levels of Learning are:

- Unconscious Incompetence
- Conscious Incompetence
- Conscious Competence
- Unconscious Competence

(Note: when you are self-aware that you are at an unconscious competence stage, doesn't that mean there is a fifth level?)

More simply put, these levels are

- Unconscious Incompetence = You are unaware about something.
- Conscious Incompetence = You become cognizant of your ignorance.
- Conscious Competence = You learn new information or skills and practice them so you are not stupid.
- Unconscious Competence = The skills are part of you and your life—second nature. You don't even think about them. We become slaves to our habits.

Charismatic traits and skills can be the same. Some you may already have and apply. You caught your spouse after all or won that job. Can you become more magnetic? What are the skills that can make your personality seem bigger?

The following pages will explore the world of personal charisma. Some of these skills might be new to you. Others are already part of your body language, speech, or listening skills. Perhaps your own behaviors were gleaned from a parent, or taught by a teacher, admired in a mentor, or even just trial and error. When first developed during the conscious competence stage, these new skills may feel uncomfortable.

As you try a new listening behavior, you might find it well received. "Well, that was cool. I will try that again and see if it works with others." After the third or fourth success, it starts to become habitual, unconsciously seeping into your DNA.

How powerful are these skills? Can they manipulate? Unfortunately, they can. It is easy to point to a Hitler or Jim Jones and the horror of Jonestown to see the power of influence. Know that true long-term change and significance will not come if these skills are used for immoral or selfish reasons. Eventually, people can sense manipulation. Others can tell the difference between authentic and fake. There is a difference between being "sold" and wanting to buy.

Some of the following charisma skills might work for you. Some may not. Most will make you a more powerful presenter, a better listener, and a more inspiring leader. There are things

you should be doing anyway as you read on.

The Charisma Pyramid

Since charisma is assigned by the customer (i.e., follower, stakeholder, friend, family) these skills have been classified into three groups: See, Hear, and Feel.

The first two aspects of personal charisma match up with the often-misinterpreted study[37] on likeability by Albert Mehrabian, a professor of psychology at UCLA. His work postulates that when three elements of communication are congruent, then a meaningful connection occurs, which he calls Likability.

$$\text{Total Liking} = 7\% \text{ Verbal Liking} + 38\% \text{ Vocal Liking} + 55\% \text{ Facial Liking}$$

Mehrabian's three measurables, (often called the 3V's - verbal, vocal, & visual) are parts of the See and Hear of personal charisma. The Total Liking aspect is what we Feel, the third part of personal charisma.

See Charisma

The Biggest Gorilla in the Room

Charismatic people seem bigger than life because they occupy more space. They have physical behaviors that make them seem more powerful, imposing and even magical. We naturally have a comfort zone, determined by country, society, wealth, and physical size. 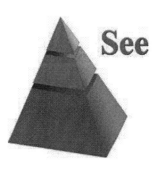 Regardless, there is an ability to command more space than an average person.

Try this experiment. Next time you walk in a public place, mentally pull on an imaginary string that is protruding from the top of your head so that you stand more erect, throwback your shoulders, raise your chin, and straighten your back. Take purposeful steps and think, "I own the three to four feet around me." As you walk, those in proximity visually scan their environment and will subconsciously give you "biggest gorilla" status. People will literally move aside as you approach. Subconsciously, they measure those around them and give an alpha dog judgment, often without even being aware of their actions.

In the bushes in front of my house are several garden snakes that enjoy an abundance of chipmunks. We have chosen to give all of the snakes the common name of Russell. When working on the landscape there have been times when I heard a "Russell in the bushes" and instinctively react with a start. Even though I know the snakes to be harmless, they still invoke a response. Biggest gorilla mentality evokes this from others. We recoil at the rustle in the bushes; we respect the biggest gorilla.

Our ability to read the environment and respond by those who arrive and depart from our current setting is more powerful that we imagine. Consider the findings of psychologist Nalini Ambady. Ambady introduced the term "thin slices" to refer to the almost instantaneous non-verbal clues gleaned by college students as they determined a professor's effectiveness after watching a two-second film clip of teaching. These two-second assessments were almost identical as those given by the students who had experienced the professor for a multi-week course.[38]

Others "read" you as you enter a room or draw close for a handshake. How you carry yourself can be more powerful than words. One MIT study discovered that others would determine how successful a conversation was going just by watching a person on the phone. They did not even need to know what words were being said—all that with an 87% accuracy.[39]

We scan our environment for the various Russell's (snakes, possible threats, rewards) that communicate and interact with us. Our brains are wired for the novel or unique. Perhaps this new thing will eat us. Maybe a powerful person is passing out favors. We scan our personal radar trained on the ever so slight nuances in facial cues, body language, and power.

Judging your book by its cover

If your appearance is questionable, then the charisma may be short in coming. If you have bad breath, deal with it. Personable grooming is up to you. To quote one cartoon, "You just can't train nose hairs into a moustache." Ask a friend to give you the kind of feedback that is honest and helpful. Find someone you trust and from whom you can take serious feedback without being offended (tough to find). Expensive clothes communicate wealth and social rank. Societies ingrain their citizens to observe and assign power to those who look successful. This dates back to the Greeks and the Sophists. Today a blue suit is perceived as more powerful than a brown suit. Both can be better than a T-shirt and jeans. The scuffed shoes communicate a ton about your presence, self-respect, and control. Forest Gump said it best with, "You can tell a lot about a person by their shoes."

In one conversation my friend said, "Kordell, lose the white shirts. They wash out your face." Another said, "Cut your hair." Surprisingly the haircut got a lot of positive comments and some a little hurtful. "You needed to lose your hair "wings." (I know, with friends like these, who needs enemies?) Does how you look, even your smell, affect assigned charisma? Perhaps.

Breaking the Third Plane

There in front of the podium sits the audience. As the speaker steps out from behind the lectern and moves into the aisle that runs down the center of the room, an invisible floor to ceiling plane separates audience and speaker. At that point the speaker becomes part of the audience and the "us/them" position evaporates. The speaker can retreat back, move left or right, but the plane has been broken. A more intimate mind-set occurs in the minds of the audience. If you need to present to an audience, get out from behind the lectern. Depending on the size of the room, noise, or the size of the audience, you might have to orchestrate a handheld microphone or even a wireless lapel microphone.

There are "third planes" between us and others that will make you more charismatic as well. You find yourself sitting in the seat next to Bill, a co-worker, who has his arms on the table and hands clutching a coffee cup. It does not really matter who is talking. If you, when it is appropriate, reach over and nonchalantly touch their arm, a message is received by the other. In one study the person across the table moves from a 30%+ acceptance of you to an almost 90% acceptance because of the "intimacy" of this arm touch. As your charisma skills grow, you will find yourself becoming more comfortable. Nudging their arm with the back of your hand has the same effect.

Handshakes

A handshake is intended to break the third plane the people put around themselves. You offer your right hand to the other person. The right hand was your sword hand, so an empty hand indicated that you were with "a friend."

When I first met J. Martell Bird, he had developed the handshake to an art form. A former FBI agent and part of J. Edgar Hoover's inner circle, he had spent his life studying (and spying) on criminals, movie stars, and famous personalities. He had developed a personality that exuded warmth and intense interest in those with whom he connected. When you shook his hand, you felt magic. His was a handshake Mona Lisa.

Charisma can be locked up in your handshake. Too firm and you come across as a bully or someone who has something to prove. A soft handshake and you are not taken seriously. The key is to return a handshake in kind. How do you know the other person doesn't have severe arthritis and a firm handshake could cause pain for hours? (Now, *that* portrays warmth and presence. Not!) A handshake that envelops applies a warming squeeze and communicates "connection" is invaluable.

Find your friend and practice. Get their feedback. When you have people complimenting you on your handshake, then you have probably arrived. Women especially need this skill. Get someone to coach you. Even if you think you are fine with your handshake, it would not hurt to ask for feedback from friends or co-workers.

If you turn your hand so that it is not perpendicular after the shake, you either send the message that you are dominating (if your hand is on top) or submissive (if you hand is

on the bottom). Keep your hand perpendicular to the ground. Don't hold a cold drink in your right hand prior to a handshake at a social event. A cold, wet, and clammy handshake is not what you want to give. Raise your thumb and keep your hand flat. Don't slap their hand as you make contact. If you connect properly, you will find your index finger is almost touching their wrist. Extend your hand and notice the "V" shape of your extended thumb and your first finger. That "V" needs to make contact with the "V" in the other person's hand.

Do not vacuum in the other person once a handshake occurs. There is no reason to put your left hand on top of theirs or to reach in and grab their arm or shoulder. Unless the other person is a friend, stay away from these handshakes that have an added contact caveat. Shake from the elbow, not the wrist.

Make eye contact and a warm smile. (More on the secrets of handshake/ eye contact later.)

In one conversation with an executive on charismatic behaviors, he pushed back when I suggested he just use one hand in a handshake. Putting the left hand on top of the clasped right hands sends a message of dominance. "I don't care," he said. "I think that my left hand portrays warmth." The science would counter that. I am sure that what works for one person may not work with another.

Hands-down Tips

A large amount of your brain is dedicated to hands. Others can get a lot of information from what you do with yours. From his book, *Louder than Words: Take Your Career from Average to Exceptional with the Hidden Power of Nonverbal Intelligence,*[40] Joe Navarro gives some interesting tips on hands and how they communicate what is going on inside your head. Others may assess your confidence and caring by your hands. For example:

- When we are contented, blood flows to the hands making them warm and pliable. Stress makes our hands colder.
- When you are strong and confident, the space between your fingers grows, making your hands territorial. If you are insecure, the space shrinks.
- When you touch others with a full palm, it communicates affection. If you touch just with the fingertips, it communicates less affection.
- When you feel confident, your thumbs rise more often, especially with intertwined fingers.
- High confidence generates steepling. Get your point across with church-like steeples of fingers, especially the pointer finger. When the steeple goes away, so does the assigned confidence.

- When you rub your hands, you communicate stress—the more rubbing, the more the stress.
- Don't point with a finger. Use your whole hand with fingers extended. Picture yourself pulling an invisible rope. That closed hand with the index finger touching the midpoint of the thumb is also a great pointing gesture.
- Long fingernails on men are seen as effeminate. Nail biting is a sign of nervousness and insecurity.
- Tattoos on the hands are not very well received in the professional ranks and should be avoided, especially in medicine, law, and finance.
- Too many rings, or a pinky ring, and you will not be taken seriously.
- Too much touching of your face with your hands is distracting.

Claiming the Chair and the Space

Just how many chairs do you need to sit in? Charismatic people just take up more space. They are not rude about it. It is just an easy, comfortable way of claiming more space than a normal body would do. Deborah Gruenfeld from Stanford University says, "Powerful people sit sideways on chairs, drape their arms over the back, or appropriate two chairs by placing an arm across the back of an adjacent chair. They put their feet on the desk. They sit on the desk."[41]

When you drape your arm across the back of the chair next to you, you communicate, "I now claim the chair I am sitting in and this one next to me." If someone is sitting in that chair, does that not make them your peep? By grabbing more space, charismatic people capture others. This is almost an extension of the "biggest gorilla" quality. By locking hands and placing them behind your head while leaning back, you communicate an openness that allows you to claim more space. It also communicates an ease and comfort with the surroundings.

The Head Nod

There is a value difference assigned by others based on the speed of your head nodding up and down. The quick, up-and-down head nod communicates, "Yeah, yeah, I've got it . . . go on. Keep going." If instead you *slowly* nod your head up and down it communicates, "Ah ha. That is very interesting." It means that the listener (you) is really drinking in what the other person is saying, that you are weighing the words against their own thinking. It also communicates, "Yes, you are right." The slow head nod is more profound and makes you seem like a deeper thinker.

Futzing

To "futz" is a scientific term I used with my six children as they were growing up. Futzing is a person preoccupied with tossing something in the air, spinning something on the table in front of you, or rocking it back and forth. It is playing with, molding, spinning, tossing, flipping, interacting with, or any other activity that is either consciously or unconsciously done with "stuff." It might communicate stress or that the other person doesn't warrant full attention. It runs the gambit of biting fingernails to texting during a conversation. Research done by Dr. Glenn Wilson at King's College London shows that texting while working lowers IQ by 10 points, almost three times worse than smoking marijuana.

We will call him Kody. He is personable, motivated, very bright, and constantly futzing with things. Remember the Pixar movie *UP*? Kody is like the dog who is distracted with "squirrel" type things. He seems to be constantly "checked out," even while he is listening. Be aware of your own futzing activities. Futzing decreases your influence and power. Are there things you do that are not on the list below?

- Stop playing with the silverware. (My ex-wife is rolling her eyes on this one.)
- Leave the crystal glasses alone.
- Stop flipping your pen around your finger.
- Stop spinning your cell phone on the table top.
- Stop twirling your hair.
- Stop tapping your fingers.
- Leave the stuff alone that is on the table/desk/counter top in front of you.
- That nervous leg bounce may be unconscious, but it is communicating messages to those around you.

In his book, *What Every Body is Saying: An Ex-FBI Agent's Guide to Speed-Reading People,* Joe Navarro tells the story of one interrogation that had a person of interest responding to questions. With her legs crossed at the knee, she subconsciously bounced her top leg, her foot slightly kicking the air. When one particular question was asked, she started to nervously shake the foot back and forth. After some additional investigation, her body language "tell" resulted in her current twenty-five-year prison sentence. Your subconscious is communicating even when you sit quietly.

Mirroring

I have a friend who has extremely gifted kids. His two daughters attended Julliard as violin and cellist wizards. They have a younger brother who is studying in Germany under a master teacher after he won the Young Artists Division of the prodigious Yehudi Menuhin International Violin Competition. Chad Hoopes travels the globe playing with symphony orchestras across Europe and the United States. His mastering of the instrument is the stuff of history and legendary masters. He is the real deal.

A few years back during the Christmas holidays, I asked the three kids if they would get their instruments and play. Words cannot express the beauty of this ethereal sound. My mother was a professional pianist. My musical ear is trained to listen to their music as surreal. Tears streamed down my face. Not only were they gifted beyond description, their individual instruments combined together as a synergistic whole.

MRI research shows that when musicians play at this level, their right brains are more connected with the right brains of the other musicians than their own right brain is connected with their own left hemisphere.[42] With this in mind, the term "limbic resonance" was first coined in the book, *A General Theory of Love*, by Thomas Lewis, Fari Amini and Richard Lannon.[43] According to their research, there are oscillator neurons in the brain that reach out in an empathetic way. It seems our brains are wired to connect with others who look like us, sound like us, or even stand like us.

If you mirror the other person's many gestures, their stance, as well as other body positions and language, you start to sync with their oscillator paths. If they sit with their legs crossed, you mimic and cross your legs. If they fold their arms, you fold yours. In small ways, you slow or speed up your speech, or match their tone. You mirror their actions. As their brain unconsciously notices that you look and feel like them, trust develops in a subliminal way. Charismatic people do this without thinking, mimicking the other person, and by so doing, they build almost instant rapport. A great example is the still mysterious infection of a yawn. Just what makes you prone to follow?

This bonding accord installs a "liking" in their mind and heart. You will find them sharing more, and if you use listening skills, you will become almost mesmerizing. Try to mirror the other person with what feels natural for you. If they wave their arm, perhaps you partially raise yours. If they stand with crossed arms, perhaps you put one arm across your chest, the other arm and hand cupping your chin. Don't be afraid to do this after a little time goes by so that is seems more natural. Otherwise, you will look like a third grader playing a game.

The next time you need to return something to the store, and if you will be aware of the physical body language of the clerk and mirror it, you will be surprised at how quickly the two of you become connected. The outcomes will be more favorable. No sales slip? No problem. Do you have an irate customer? Pull out your limbic resonance skills and build a quick friendship to temper the frustration.

Moving Your Butt around the Geography

When you are intensely listening to someone—and listening is the keystone for charisma—your body covers territory. Sit in any restaurant on a Friday evening and notice the couples at other tables. I often ask audiences how you can tell the difference between dating and married couples. I hear things like:

- "Because dating couples talk to each other. Married people could care less."
- "Husband and wife are both texting."
- "Dating couples look like they are having a great time."
- "Dating couples actually look at each other."
- "You can tell that at least one person is really interesting in a dating situation."

When people "date," there can be a mutual interest that *shows*. You can *see* they are interested; it's visible. When any person is authentically listening, they tend to move their derriere around a chair. This is a slow, unconscious dance of sorts. Alternatively, they lean in. They may slide forward and then lean back. Perhaps they turn their body sideways and turn the head so one ear "doesn't miss a thing."

When you are really listening, you tend to show it physically. You will cock your head; put your chin in your hand. Maybe you put an arm across your chest and the other holding your cheek Jack Benny style.

I remind you that initially you will have to do this consciously. After a while, it will become an unconsciously competent behavior.

Listening

The summer of 1886 was especially hot in the United Kingdom, both for temperature and politics. In the strength of this Victorian period, a contest of sorts between two powerful leaders was on stage. A young lady just happened to have dinner on successive nights with the two contestants in a national election. The first night it was with the fiery and spirited William Gladstone. The next night it was with the warm and charming Benjamin Disraeli. Since control of the British Empire was at stake, the intense animosity between the two men spilled over into the public's interest.

When asked her impressions of the two men, she offered her thoughts to the newspaper.

"When I left the dining room after sitting next to Mr. Gladstone, I thought he was the cleverest man in England. But after sitting next to Mr. Disraeli, I thought I was the cleverest woman in England."

Gladstone, known for his rhetoric, had a different effect on her than the charismatic Disraeli. Disraeli created friends and planted favorable impressions with his charm. At the core of charm was the ability to listen, so much so that others felt that they were "the only person in the room." In a twist on Disraeli, you may have heard "talk to a man about himself and he will talk for hours."

The late Zig Ziglar related a story of his meeting a very knowledgeable and charming man in the community while he was a young man. When they started talking, the gentleman asked Zig about himself. They only had an hour, and the end of the time Zig said he found that he had done most of the talking. As Ziglar left, he noted that indeed the gentleman was knowledgeable because "he not only knew what he knew, but he also knew everything that I knew."

Charismatic people understand that listening is key. They have an honest ability to draw us out and make us feel like we are all that matters. The higher the focused attention we give, the greater the charisma assigned. With the speed of the brain versus the speed of the spoken word, it is natural for the mind to wander. It is almost impossible to be 100% engaged. If you can raise your attention and focus by 20% or more, the positive impact is huge.

The Eyes Have It.

What can you do with your face to communicate that you are listening? When asked, most respond with "You smile." The problem is that if the smile is not sincere, it detracts from the conversation because a smile is practically impossible to fake. A true smile comes from the heart and it is hard to feel like smiling all the time. To be authentic, a smile draws down the inside of the eyebrows and brings the mouth in a very natural way. Very hard to fake.

Another facial expression that detracts from your charisma is the furrowed brow. I heard one expert describe this as the "jail bars" that form between the eyebrows. My wife calls them "the elevens." These vertical lines that form between in the brows communicate scrutiny and intensity. They give the kind of distanced look used by police during interrogation and information gathering. Jail bars do not offer warmth. The talking person has to ask, "Are they intensely listening or are they disagreeing with my thoughts?"

So what works? What kind of new skills learned and practiced will communicate that you are sincerely listening? It is in the eyes and the three inches above them—the eyes, the eye brows and the forehead. The secret to putting on a listening face is in that area right above the eyebrows. When you are listening, your eyebrows arch upward in an expression that says, "Really? Are you kidding me? Seriously?" This tends to put wrinkles across the forehead. Your jail bars from a furrowed brown vanish.

Evaluate your own face. When you are listening to an interesting story, you will catch your own eyebrows arching upward. Some people even have a talent to raise just one eye brow. You can also get this facial 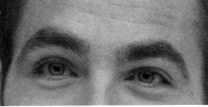 expression by dropping your chin slightly and looking upward like you were looking over the top of glasses. At first, you will find this somewhat foreign. With practice, however, you will find others wanting to talk to you. They will share things that are beyond a normal conversation.

The Stare

There is real science to star-crossed lovers who look deeply into one another's eyes. When those dating couples lean forward and talk, they are playing with real chemistry. In one study, participants were to look at one another's eyes and count the blinks. The counting was really a way of getting them to make intense eye connection without the awkwardness usually associated with this looking deeply into another's gaze. The results were measurable increases in affection and passion toward the person who was connecting eye to eye.[44]

According to the anthropologist Helen Fisher, the act of staring intensely into the eyes can release a chemical called phenethylamine into the nervous system. This chemical, often referred to as PEA, drives up the heart rate and produces the same effect of those who fall in love.

When your eyes wander during a conversation, you send a message that you are not listening deeply and that you are missing a chance to connect at a deeply emotional state. Think chocolate. The effect from chocolate on the body is similar to the deep stare. Both incite PEA hormone production.

The Departing Look

As your charismatic "look" skills improve and you become more magnetic, there will be a time when your departure creates a certain regret or sorrow in the other. Think of the grief experienced after the loss of a loved one. On a minor scale, the departing charismatic creates a similar grief. To combat that before leaving, maintain eye contact for three seconds, then there is less separation distress.

Summary

- Be the biggest gorilla in the room.
- Break the third plane.
- Handshakes are important.
- Work on your clothes.
- Be aware of your hands and what they communicate.
- Occupy more space.
- Don't futz with things in your environment.

- Mirror the body language of those to whom you are speaking.
- Move your posterior around, shift your weight to communicate listening.
- If you are going to nod your head, make it a slow, deliberate nod.
- A deliberate and intense stare can release hormones in the other person that mimic love at first sight.

Hear Charisma

If you watch two dogs approach each other, there are all sorts of messages going back and forth. We humans do the same thing with our voices when we communicate. When a dog's owner comes home, there is an excitement of connection for the dog. The pet will jump up on the master, wagging the tail vigorously. There might even be a high-pitched whine of happiness. Dogs tend to smile with their whole body.

On the other hand, when a dog wants to communicate power or control, the verbal registry drops, sometimes even a growl. When humans smile, muscles in the face and throat tighten and makes the tone of voice go up.  Like the happy dog, it communicates excitement and happiness. In the Provence region of France, the local dialects there take on a more lilting tone, almost a singsong quality. Could this be why foreigners find this area so friendly? A smiling "voice," although happy, lacks in influence and power. The lower registers of voice, like a growl, communicate Chutzpah, presence and gravitas.

That is why the smiling face may not always be the most charismatic expression. Instead, the tone drop of a lowered voice becomes deliberate and measured. These phenomena communicate an intensity of interest and attention to the things at hand. Think of the growl without the threat.

Down Talk and Up Talk

When two women meet, often there is a common pitch to their sentences.

"How are you? And your kids?" The tone is lilting, light and friendly. Often the sentences end with a rise in the tone of voice toward the end. The intent is to connect and be non-threatening. When two women meet, should the tone of voice be in the lower registries, initially communications between them is more guarded.

For men, the lower registers of their voice are more charismatic, especially when there is some contrast with higher pitched phrases. "In three languages, I see a similar pattern," says Jody Kreiman, a voice expert at the UCLA David Geffen School of Medicine. "My research shows that charismatic leaders of any type in any culture tend to stretch their voice to the lower and higher limits during a public speech, which is the most important and risky context of communication for leadership."[45] The ability to use your voice like an entertainer is a skill.

Getting a Drop on the Final Word

On YouTube, you can do a search on Brad Pitt interviews. If you watch an interview for *A River Runs through It*, you will hear a young Brad Pitt answer questions in a higher-toned voice with an excitement that is reminiscent of the dog with the wagging tail. When asked a question about director Robert Redford, his response ends in an ascending tone on the final words. He ends his sentences on a raised tone. This is not charismatic.

Now, go back to YouTube to view an interview with the modern Pitt. You find a slower delivery. You will also notice one very different behavior as well. On the last word of a sentence the tone of Mr. Pitt's voice drops. In the earlier interview, his voice rose (tail wag), but now the tone on the last word drops (grrrrrrr) to the registers where someone who wants to be taken seriously dwells. Charisma grows when there is a tone drop on the last word of the sentence.

Wizard of Pause

Those who are charismatic pause in their sentences. They do not speak slowly but intentionally put pauses into their phrases. "I feel (pause) that there is a (pause) serious issue here (tone drop)." You would think that these pauses would cause the listener's mind to wander. Pauses in word delivery give the listener time to internalize what the message is. They also think about how the information pertains to their world.

The Two-Second Response Pause

When asked a question, the charismatic person can wait a moment before answering. The unspoken message here is that they are in charge and what they are going to say is meaningful and valuable.

People Love to Be Asked their Opinions.

Several years ago, a representative of the Ohio Board of Regents came to me with a request. "If we gave you the materials in a sales course we bought for some of the universities in the state, could you help us ramp up our sales-training offerings?" I looked at the material and realized that it, like most information, was not something people would put into practice. Sure, they would read it. But would they use it?

Years ago, I was immersed in the methodology of David Sibbet and his Grove Consulting International. "The Grove" uses a process that gets all in a group involved in the planning, meeting, or discussion using large wall-sized charts. As people add views on a subject, a "graphic facilitator" records information with words and pictures on paper or whiteboards. The process gets high participation and consensus on outcomes.

What would happen if I combined the new sales training concepts with the Grove Consulting practices? Consequently, I wrote a book and have seen sales teams across the country discover a new way of selling with the kind of consultative skills of professionals—doctors, lawyers and therapists.

What does this have to do with charisma? People love to hear questions, especially if they know the answers. So how do you use this to become more charismatic? Ask questions! Today your value is not the information you know; it is the questions you ask. Great leaders and coaches know team dynamics lead to questions that, unless answered, will stymie the progress of the team. If a new coach arrives, then the same questions occur in the minds of the team. If a new employee is added to the team, the following questions occur:

- Why are we here? (What is the agenda?)
- Who are you? (Can I trust you?)
- What are we going to do? (Goals for the group)
- How are we going to do those? (Buy-in and resources to get the job done)
- Who is going to do what, when, and how? (Execution)

Remember, every time the team changes (or a new strategic plan is needed) then the group needs to work through the questions.

Another set of questions are part of sales (or part of every networking meeting, Christmas party, or social activity):

- Who are you? (Tell me about your world.)
- What are your biggest challenges?

- How are those challenges growing into bigger problems?
- What do you think the solution to the problems should look like?

Charisma asks questions of your followers, customers, and loved ones. Then it listens intensely. There are visual, verbal and emotion cues to make this intense listening improve.

Feel Charisma

He was a conservative sort and yet a real scamp. Even his eyes had that maverick, whimsical, look of mischief. Al Williams, referenced before, was not the definition of a fine physical specimen. He was short and somewhat stocky, with wavy reddish hair, combed straight back, and his dark-rimmed glasses with thick lenses magnified the intensity of his glance. His freckled complexion and diminutive physical presence would remind you of a larger version of Gimli, the dwarf member of *Fellowship of the Ring,* without the abundance of hair. His was not a legacy of conquering countries or balance sheets. His heritage? He was the misfit that launched no-name generic food products in the United States in the late 1970s. Williams single-handedly (and with a few accomplices, myself included) waged war on some of the biggest corporations in the United States.

For the uninitiated, no-name generics were stark white packages with black font descriptions of simple products at prices below the big, fat national brands. When you picked up a can, the label proclaimed a simple "corn." The lack of packaging, marketing, and standard quality products would save a nickel here and a dime there. The savings would climb as you purchased sibling products in cleaning supplies, baking products, and so forth.

The short-lived, no-name generics phenomenon had Ivy League executives with prodigious diplomas on the wall at a quandary. There was no army of minion sales people. Yet, the products weaseled their way onto grocery shelves across the country. In a time of financial downturn, whole aisles magically materialized throughout stores across the country of these plain, white packaged goods.

Nearly thirty years later the author met a former product manager who had worked for Proctor & Gamble during that time. When the conversation came up about no-name generics, she was still visibly angry at the havoc they caused in her career decades earlier. At the center of the revolution was the charismatic character, Al Williams. He would be considered a true no-name. He never made the news. He went out of his way to refrain from broadcasting who he was or what he was doing to others. "If they find out that you are the person behind their misery, your competition will be watching you. Better to show up out of nowhere and have them scratch their heads asking, "What happened?"

In the face of normality and Thermopylaen like opposition, Al Williams had this down to earth, "aw shucks" honesty that instilled a "We *can* take that hill" belief. Most of all, Al Williams had presence. His natural warmth was something that you *felt*. It drove out doubt and bolstered self-will. When you had a conversation, you did not think he listened to you; you *knew* he listened to you. You *felt* cared about.

There is a reason that **Feel** is represented by the bottom two-thirds of the personal charisma pyramid. By volume, **Feel** makes up 80% of charisma. What the person sees or hears from you has only a 20% impact. Real charisma power is in the **Feel.**

As the world increases in speed and choices multiply, people rely more and more on emotion and their gut feel. From Olivia Fox Cabane we read:

> "Charisma, which makes us *feel* impressed, inspired, or thrillingly special, speaks to our emotional side. It bypasses our logical thinking. Just as the feeling of awe goes beyond our understanding and touches us at an emotional level, so does charisma."[46]

Charisma then magnifies the logical. Research shows that a good performance review given without charisma is not received as well as a bad performance review given *with* charisma. It seems that bedside manners can trump clinical competence. People sue a technically correct doctor who is inept in their interpersonal skills a lot more than they do a friendly, attentive doctor. You can kill the customer, and if they like you, then your malpractice costs are less.

In the 1980s and 1990s a team of scientists at the University of Parma in Italy discovered the aforementioned mirror neurons.[47] These special cells in the brains of studied monkeys indicate that certain cells mirror or mimic the actions of others. Humans have these mirror neurons as well, and speculation is that we mirror the thoughts, actions, and feelings of others in special portions of the inferior frontal cortex and superior parietal lobes. In short, charisma is contagious. How you feel about a person is easily experienced by others. Not only does charisma make the harsh more palatable but also others' sense the feelings of their peers, and so they too join in the fun.

Mr. Spock would say, "That is not logical." Charisma trumps logic. We really do believe in dreams and a forward vision—that valuable currency of charisma. "Where there is no vision the people perish."[48] At the heart of dreams, hopes, and passion is feeling. You can practice raising your eyebrows or orchestrating your voice, but you cannot counterfeit the feeling component.

Personal warmth is the core of charisma. Magical and surreal, its very essence is indeed hard to pinpoint. One charisma observation is, "Well, since she seems to have it and I can't seem to identify it, I guess it is something that you are born with, because I sure feel it when I am around her."

If you want others to feel your warmth, regardless of introvert or extrovert styles, you need to go back to the word charity. This divine version of love is bigger than life. People feel it. We all have natural radar built into our deep-seated instincts that naturally look for fight or flight threats. The opposite, and just as palpable, is that trust that comes from someone who has personal presence, the warmth of heart, and a true caring for us.

Feel charisma is an inward thing, a spiritual event. Love is felt. Presence of character in others is sensed beyond what we see or hear.

We are not physical beings having a spiritual experience; we are spiritual beings having a physical experience.

PIERRE TEILHARD DE CHARDIN

How do you increase your personal warmth? How do you increase your skills of presence or love? What are the skills, those internal mental practices that make up this very essence of personal charisma?

Magic at 35,000 Feet

The flight leveled off at a cruising altitude for the journey to Australia. In my lap was the package, its gift wrapping giving way to reveal a life-changing book for myself and thousands of others. The time was decades ago. Little did I know that the simple and sublime skills outlined in that book were written by my own personal coach to develop a modicum of personal charisma. Strangely new at first but with practice, I found new abilities to influence and persuade from the pages. The book was *The Greatest Salesman in the World* by Og Mandino. With solid practices for those who want to persuade others, this book was the perfect primer for a young person.

In midst of the Mandino story were ten scrolls, each with a selling principle. Central stage of the ten scrolls was the second one, which has become known as the "Love Scroll." For the uninitiated, the book asked you to read each scroll (concept) three times a day, "so that it magically becomes part of you and your thinking." It did not take long to feel the magic of putting the Love Scroll into practice. Hesitant at first, then with success upon favorable success, confidence increased as others sensed the warmth and love created with these principles.

Praise

We work so we can get money to buy nice clothes and to get the respect of those around us. We write the book, prepare the speech, work the sixty-hour weeks to impress and influence others. Why? What do we get out of our efforts? Money? Fame? Love? Power? We go to great efforts to pursue those things that we see as valuable.

What happens if we let go of our own pursuits and instead focus on the deep needs of others? Why hold out on giving them something called recognition? Is there some limited inventory for recognition, and you are rationing it out so you do not run out before you die? In the quiet lives of desperation experienced by others, there is a cooling liquid that you can freely provide. Is your motive to manipulate? If so, turn back to the first part of the book and start over. Your motive is to lift . . . to love.

Percy Whiting was a contemporary of Dale Carnegie. Whiting wrote the original sales book for Dale Carnegie training. In one story, he relates making a sales call with a new salesperson. As they were greeting the receptionist, Percy complimented her fingernails. As they found a seat while waiting for their appointment, the salesperson quizzed Whiting on his motivation and method for complimenting the receptionist. "There was no ulterior motive," Whiting responded. She had beautiful fingernails."

I watched them tearing a building down,
A gang of men in a busy town.
With a ho-heave-ho and lusty yell,
They swung a beam and a sidewall fell.
I asked the foreman, "Are these men skilled,
As the men you'd hire if you had to build?"
He gave me a laugh and said, "No indeed!
Just common labor is all I need.
I can easily wreck in a day or two
What builders have taken a year to do.
And I tho't to myself as I went my way,
Which of these two roles have I tried to play?
Am I a builder who works with care,
Measuring life by the rule and square?
Am I shaping my deeds by a well-made plan,
Patiently doing the best I can?
Or am I a wrecker who walks the town,
Content with the labor of tearing down?
(Author Unknown)

Appreciation and Gratitude

Others assign charisma. They define it. When they feel that you value what they think, feel and do, then trust, like the plant from the seed, it erupts. Everyone has something that is worthy of your attention. *The road to personal charisma presence travels through the wilderness of gratitude* before it gets to charity.

In order to praise others you must first master appreciation and gratitude. The first step is to seek out their unique and valuable qualities and values. If you can't see them, then slow down. Trust that as you put your own personal interests aside and focus on others, you are going the right direction.

People are suspicious of others. They hide behind walls of uncertainty. Your pursuit of discovering the gifts, abilities, and work of others will allow magical connections to occur. The recent success of Tom Rath's book, *Strengths Finder,* looks at the value in others. People get a real buzz when they are recognized and appreciated for their individual worth.

To get personal charisma means appreciating and loving other people. Look for the great qualities that each person uniquely offers. Gratitude takes us to a place where we can look on others with a caring heart. Consider . . .

> We love the
> **Artist** for their eye for beauty
> **Analytic** for the safety they bring
> **Intelligent** for their unique perspectives
> **Simpler Minds** for the innocence they possess
> **Beautiful** for their eyes of sadness
> **Ugly** for their souls of peace
> **Old** for the wisdom they can share
> **Young** for their faith

Strong for the loads they carry
Weak for the service we can provide
Famous for the entertainment they share
Ordinary for the complexity of life
Rich for they are still human
Poor for they are divine

When you combine appreciation, gratitude and praise . . . look out! Life becomes very exciting. The world will shower you with gifts when you do this. You will find yourself getting extra French fries without asking. To praise and be grateful will fill your world with free room upgrades. You will make the sun break through the clouds in another person's day.

Start small. The Pied Piper had to practice before his magic skills occurred. Develop your listening muscles. Let your conversations center more on others and their world. It's OK to talk about yourself, but listening to others, building them up, having your own understanding broadened will set you apart. It will make you charismatic.

Greetings and connections

Perhaps the single most powerful thing you can do is in unspoken communications with others. In the business world, the "touchy, feely" is shunned. If you will put aside scientific methods for a moment and assume that maybe, just maybe, there might be an influence, a power, an energy from which you could benefit, I guarantee you a life-changing skill.

Recent science has a hard time explaining how atoms divide from one another by space in the lab, and yet the atoms still behave physically as if they were next to each other. Like the connection between atoms, there is a spiritual connection that occurs between people. When you try the following, you too can experience this mystical and mesmerizing phenomenon.

Here is how it works. When you meet someone, simply look them in the eye, and in silence to yourself say, "I love you." I first tried this over forty years ago after reading Og Mandino's book. It works. You too will experience as it helps lift and connect almost instantly.

I was recently walking through a big-box home improvement store with my remodeling contractor. One of the store's "experts" approached us to see if we needed help. I "turned on" this internal greeting. Instantaneously the store expert became a friend. After several minutes, the contractor interrupted. "Do you two know each other?"

"No, we just met."

As we finished the conversation and walked down the aisle, the contractor turned and said, "That was incredible. How did you do that?"

In due course, the ability to connect with others at this "spiritual" level will become stronger. Like unconscious competent skills, ultimately you will forget that you even connect this way. Does it work every time? Not always. But as you perfect these skills, it makes each human interaction a wonderful gift for you and the other person.

Loving Self

To react with warmth, you must love yourself. *Feel* charisma requires personal development and inward inspection (as cement added to sand, rock, and water) to create a solid foundation. Honesty travels arm in arm with trust. Trust is the foundation for love. Love, in its authentic form, becomes charisma. You cannot hide the undisciplined soul. The striving heart calls out with unspoken words . . . feelings.

That which we are, we shall teach, not voluntarily, but involuntarily.

RALPH WALDO EMERSON

In Conclusion

There are no shortcuts for inspecting and improving your life. What are you consuming with your mind as well as with your mouth? Are you consuming? Is it the trivial, mindless drivel pandered by modern media? These unabated recreations create gluttons. "Feel" charisma requires you to sacrifice self. You don't "get" charisma; you must give away to possess it. Conversations are not about you. They are about others. Praise is not given because you want to lift others, not because you want to manipulate. The parent praises the child out of love. Praise is for others because they need it and deserve it. Often nothing is in it for you. So, why would you do this? Feel charisma is personal presence that will grow in its depth and can (and should) be your gift and contribution to the universe.

Significance

Who has been significant in your life? Parents, spouses, friends, teachers, and other role models all help you shape your life. They helped you with the massive transitions that occurred at marriage, graduation, the arrival of kids, and even the loss of loved ones. They have a vested interest in you with their care and love. We starve for this connectedness. It is a divine gift. It is charismatic.

Charisma is both for you and your business. It is Steve Jobs telling his would-be recruit, John Scully, "Do you want to sell sugared water or do you want to change the world? It brings the impact of Gandhi, the joy of Disney or the creative unleashing of genius using an Apple computer product. Make a difference. Be significant.

Up your game. Improve yourself and others through an increase in charisma. Charisma with its building and lifting will bring personal fulfillment. The brilliance of a rising sun is like the breaking light of charisma. Your new horizons wait.

Appendix A

The Charisma Survey

In 2004, my business started helping educators, corporations, associations, and government. We provided a consultant role to assist clients to move past customer service and into creating *customer experience*. Hundreds of clients and tens of thousands of audience members were asking for what comes after the customer experience. In 2013 and 2014, we conducted surveys and interviews of thousands of individuals asking some basic questions:

- What organizations would you identify as above all their competition?
- Why?

After looking at the answers, we eventually settled on a common word for these magical businesses: **charismatic.** They had a personality, warmth, and a relationship that went beyond mere words.

In 2014, we initiated more surveys in connection with group presentations to association executives, chambers of commerce, convention and conference audiences and consulting engagements with individual organizations. The cross-section of the respondents, although not scientific, was male/female, intergenerational, non-racial in mix, with individuals in low, middle, and high-income groups.

The questions were simple and elicited over 1,000 responses:

- Can a business be charismatic?
- Which organizations would you identify as charismatic?
- What is it that makes them charismatic?

According to the survey, the top 14 organizations were:

1. Disney
2. Apple
3. Starbucks
4. Southwest Airlines
5. Cirque du Soleil
6. The Beatles
7. Victoria's Secret
8. Ritz-Carlton
9. Chipotle
10. Harley-Davidson
11. Zappos
12. Blue Man Group
13. Five Guys Hamburgers and Fries
14. Dyson

Honorable mentions included: Costco, Amazon, Jimmy John's, Whole Foods, Tiffany, Costco, Panera, Virgin Airlines, Cabela's, Amano Chocolate, Panera, Wendy's of Cleveland, The Seidman Cancer Center, Gerber Poultry, IBM, Coca-Cola, Pixar, Google, IKEA, Nike, and BMW.

Appendix B

The Origins of Business Charisma

Jim Gilmore was a plucky consultant to the technology company that I worked for in the 1990s. His ability to get others out of the box made him magic with a room of executives. Years later, I read a paradigm-shifting article in the *Harvard Business Review* and later a book, *Experience Economy*. Imagine the double surprise to discover that Jim Gilmore was co-author of the concept of businesses moving into the experience economy. Consider chocolate.

Chocolate grows up.

A hundred years ago chocolate was all about the cocoa bean. Then Milton Hershey discovered how to combine (evaporated) milk, cocoa, cocoa butter (oil) and a good dose of sugar. The chocolate bar was born.[4950] The cocoa bean commodity turned into a manufactured package of joy.

Eventually, the manufactured chocolate product moved upstream with the sophistication of a box of See's or Godiva chocolates. The end goal is winning the affection of your loved one with these specialty chocolates as they create a deeper meaning, providing a hoped-for romantic statement.

There is even a more complex chocolate offering in Times Square or the Las Vegas M&M store on the strip. Here you can pay five dollars to get a customized bag of M&Ms that would cost you a dollar at the local store. There is the fun of your own personalized blend of colors to commemorate the Times Square experience takes chocolate to a higher level.

> "There, there . . . little luxury, don't you cry. You will become a necessity by and by."

In their book, *The Experience Economy*, authors Joseph Pine and Jim Gilmore chronicled their view of the dynamics of these market changes.

Commodity > Package Goods Manufacturing > Services > Experiences

The commodities of the early twentieth century migrated to the powerful packaged goods of the ' 50s, ' 60s, and ' 70s. By the ' 90s, services outranked manufacturing in the number of business offerings in the United States. Added services to the standard package gave business a tool to charge for extra value. The message sent: You may not be able to get out of the doghouse with a piece of expensive jewelry, but you can afford a gold box of chocolate that might do the job.

For coffee, the progression of business looks like this:
- Commodity = Coffee Beans
- Packaged/Manufactured = Folgers
- Service = Starbucks
- Experience = Sidewalk café in Paris

For ice cream the business offerings progressions look like this:
- Commodity = Vanilla ice cream, homemade on the farm
- Packaged/Manufactured = Chocolate/Vanilla/Strawberry
- Service = Baskin & Robbins' 31 Flavors
- Experience = 1,000 flavors (Cold Stone Creamery)

Commodity > Package Goods Manufacturing > Services > Experiences

Cocoa Beans 〉 Hershey Chocolate 〉 Godiva 〉 M&M Store

Is there something past the experience? Mathew Dixon and Brent Adamson point out in *The Challenger Sale,*[51] that 75% of all participants in their study wanted to move to the higher-value-added offerings and methods of business.[52] Jim Gilmore[53] indicated that he and his partner were already postulating what comes after an experience.

Amano Chocolate

I am pushed hard into the leather seats of the Porsche as the high performance engine exerts its influence with G force punctuation. As a corner is rounded, Mitch Burton (See Personal Charisma.) announces, "You need some chocolate." Turns are made, re-entry occurs and the parking lot is found. We find the appropriate aisle where he purchases the entire inventory of Montanya chocolate (a particular flavor of chocolate bar) that is created by Amano Artisan Chocolates. Several hundreds of dollars spent, I was back in the Porsche breaking open the "Hershey-bar-sized" box to reveal the gold foil wrapped chocolate. Willy Wonka would be so proud.

Side-bar note (no pun intended). In my younger days, I was a chocolate sales representative. In R & D and quality control kitchens of some of the largest chocolate enterprises in the US, I have tasted the finest (and cheapest) of what could be legally termed chocolate. As we sampled the Amano chocolate, I experienced something very new. Like a fine wine, this chocolate had nuances of orange, almonds, and other exotic flavors.

Art Pollard, the head chocolatier of Amano, travels the world to buy cocoa beans from remote and exotic locales. At the time of my first phone call for an interview, he was traveling by boat down the west coast of South America where he would "be out of reach of communication for a week or so."

When Art comes back to his little manufacturing plant, he blends these pure, unique cocoa beans from non-traditional locations in Madagascar, New Guinea, and the deepest, darkest realms of Mordor (Do Hobbits eat chocolate?). Each contributes to the taste experience with the unique flavors of that part of the world.

The result is chocolate that cost ten times the price of a common drugstore bar. Browse the Amano website and you will find pages of instructions on how to cleanse your palate before enjoying. You will receive instruction on how to recognize differences that affect the cocoa beans, like the amount of sun during the day, rainfall, and soil conditions. You are encouraged to have tasting parties with friends (an experience for sure).

Art Pollard is unassuming. Tall and lean, with a shock of brown hair, he is almost disarming in his down-to-earth manners. His enthusiasm for his product is infectious. You would not expect him to be the force behind more than one hundred international awards in the past seven years.

So, what is it about Amano chocolate that makes it so mesmerizing? Is it Art Pollard? Is it the packaging or the quality of the brown stuff in the middle? It is a combination of all of the above and more. Amano has charisma. Their chocolate possesses several of the eight qualities of a charismatic business. In each economic step (from commodities, packaged goods, etc.) there is an increase in the price for the offering. Charisma is a place where you move past products, services and into customer experience. It is a state where the competition fades behind, where leaders rise above managers. It is vision and hope. It is magic . . . and it is profitable.

Appendix C

The Bankruptcy Gap

"There is a light at the end of the tunnel and it is an oncoming train." They did not see it coming. Two competitors were so locked in battle that they were blindsided.

Montgomery Ward and Sears Roebuck missed the oncoming

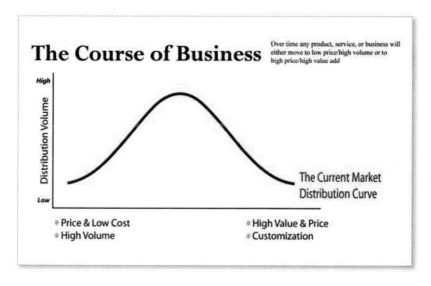

The Course of Business — Over time any product, service, or business will either move to low price/high volume or to high price/high value add

Distribution Volume (High / Low)

The Current Market Distribution Curve

- Price & Low Cost
- High Volume

- High Value & Price
- Customization

changes. So focused on each other were they that they did not see that their businesses were in serious trouble. At the high end, Nordstrom's shot them with their superior customer service, and at the low end the howitzer of Wal-Mart ambushed them. Does everyone eventually get bushwhacked by changes in their industry? What about retailers, laundry soap, travel agents, computers and *possibly* you? What do they have in common with Sears? The answer is: The Bankruptcy Gap. There was at one time only one Tide laundry detergent. Just a few months ago I counted over seventy sizes, types, and smells of Tide at the supermarket. Likewise, there are many versions of washing machines, including top-loaders, front loaders, a version for smelly clothes, for whites, and even a version in a dispensing tube so you can get the coffee stain off the front of your shirt while at the office. Diversification came about as a means to falling victim to the bankruptcy gap.

Who would go to a travel agent these days? They have gone the way of the 8 mm camera and Betamax. Newspapers seem to be the next to fall.

These are all examples of the bankruptcy gap. When you look at any market there is a bell curve for the distribution. (See above chart.) Most customers buy like Goldilocks. They don't like it too cold or too hot. They want it just right . . . in the middle. At the low end of the curve are the low price/high volume products and services. At the high end on the right side of the curve can be found the high value and customized offerings. Most of the volume is on the standard sedan, the number 1 soap in the category, the insurance policy . . . the big bump in the middle.

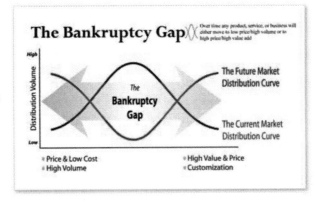

Gradually, as the competition increases, the biggest part of the curve inverts itself. This gap inversion is caused as the products and services become either more of a commodity with the customer opting for a lower price (a move to the left) or their products become tailor-made, luxury-oriented, customized, or more experience-based (a move to the right).

The $20 Papermate pen in the middle is replaced by the 10 cent Bic pen on the left, or the $250 Mont Blanc pen on the right. Both can sign a document but the Mont Blanc pen does it with more class.

What does that say about your business? Where do you need to position your offerings in the market?

According to research done by Matthew Dixon and Brent Adamson, 70% of business organizations are moving to the right. They are focused on:

- High Value
- Higher Price
- Customized products
- Creating the experience

Why wouldn't you build the high-value offering? Being eclectic and reinventing is a must. So what is keeping you from turning into new paths? The short answer is "You." Or you could just wait for the arrival of the coming train. As it runs you over, you should be able to look up and see a name emblazoned across the engine. There it plainly states: **Charisma**.

End Notes

[1] Duhigg, Charles. *The Power of Habit: Why We Do What We Do in Life and Business.* (New York: Random House, 2012), xvi.

[2] Gilmore, James H., and B. Joseph Pine II. *The Experience Economy: Work Is Theater & Every Business a Stage* (Boston, Massachusetts, Harvard Business School Press)

[4] Weber, Max. *The Theory of Social and Economic Organization.* (New York: Free Press,1947).

[5] Thibaudeau, Antoine Claire. *Mémoires sur le Consulat: 1799 à 1804.* (Paris: Chez Ponthieu et Cie, 1827), 83–84.

[6] King James Bible: Matthew 22:14

[7] Reichheld, Fred. *The Ultimate Question: Driving Good Profits and True Growth.* (Boston Massachusetts: Harvard Business School Press, 2011), 15.

[8] Neumeier, Marty. *The Brand Gap: How to Bridge the Distance Between Business Strategy and Design.* (Berkeley, California: New Riders, 2006), 19.

[9] Ibid.

[10] Dixon, Matthew, and Brent Adamson. *The Challenger Sale:Taking Control of the Customer Conversation.* (New York: Penguin Group, 2011), 7.

[11] Hogshead, Sally. *Fascinate - Your 7 Triggers to Persuasion and Captivation.* (New York: HarperCollins: 2010).

[12] Reichheld, *Ultimate Question.*

[13] Cabane, Olivia Fox. *The Charisma Myth: How Anyone Can Master the Art and Science of Personal Magnetism.* (New York: Portfolio/Penguin Group, 2013).

[14] Catmull, Edwin. Creativity Inc.: *Overcoming the Unseen Forces that Stand in the Way of True Inspiration.* (New York: Random House, 2014), 277.

[15] Reichheld, *The Ultimate Question.*

[16] Blackman, Andrew. "Can Money Buy You Happiness?" (New York: *Wall Street Journal*, November 10, 2014).

[17] King James Bible: Matthew 22:14

[18] Holden, Jim. *Power Based Selling – Confessions of an Ivy League Street Fighter.* (New York: John Wiley & Sons, 1999).

[19] Lipp, Doug. *Disney U: How the Disney University Develops the World's Most Engaged, Loyal, and Customer-Centric Employees,* 2013, (New York: McGraw Hill), 83.

[20] Simmons, Annette. The *Story Factor: Inspiration, Influence, And Persuasion Through The Art of Storytelling,* (Cambridge, MA: Basic Books, 2001), 3.

[21] Ibid.

[22] King James Bible: Mark 4:2.

[23] McKee, Robert. *Story: Substance, Structure, Style, and the Principles of Screenwriting* (New York: Harper Collins, 1997).

[24] King James Bible: Matthew 13:10-11.

[25] Dixon, *The Challenger Sale.*

[26] Frost, Robert. "The Road Not Taken." (Chicago: Holt Paperbacks, 2002).

[27] Shakespeare. *Julius Caesar*, Act 4, Scene 3.

[28] Berman, Dennis K. *10 Years Later: The $400 Billion Epistle*, (New York: The Wall Street Journal, August 19, 2014).

[29] Donlon, J.P. "How Bob Iger Remade the House that Walt Built." *Chief Executive Magazine* - July/August 2014, (Greenwich, CT: Chief Executive Group, LLC), 26.

[30] Schein, Edgar. *Organizational Culture and Leadership*. (London: Jossey-Bass, 2010).

[31] Wagner, Rodd and James K. Harter. *12: The Elements of Great Managing*. (New York: Gallup
Press, 2006).

[32] Patterson, Kerry, et al. *Change Anything: The New Science of Personal Success*, 2012, (New York: Business Plus, 2012).

[33] Harris, Dan. *Ten % Happier*, 2014 (New York, NY, HarperCollins) p. 184-185

[34] Gladwell, Malcolm. *Blink The Power of Thinking Without Thinking*. (New York: Back Bay Books/Little, Brown & Co., 2015), 40-43.

[35] Michelli, Joseph A. *The New Gold Standard: 5 Leadership Principles for Creating a Legendary Customer Experience Courtesy of the Ritz-Carlton Hotel Company* (New York: McGraw Hill, 2008), 7-8.

[36] Recounted by Robert Stein, then editor of *Redbook* in *American Heritage Magazine*, Nov/Dec 2005.

[37] Mehrabian, Albert, and Morton Wiener. "Decoding of Inconsistent Communications." *Journal of Personality and Social Psychology* 6 (1), 1967: 109–114.

[38] Ambady, Nalini, and Robert Rosenthal (1992). "Thin Slices of Expressive Behavior as Predictors of Interpersonal. Consequences: A Meta-Analysis." *Psychological Bulletin* 3 (2): 266–274. Retrieved 30 October 2013.

[39] Pentland, Alex. *Honest Signals: How They Shape Our World* (Cambridge, MA: MIT Press, 2008).

[40] Navarro, Joe. *Louder Than Words: Take Your Career from Average to Exceptional with the Hidden Power of Nonverbal Intelligence*, (New York: HarperCollins, 2010).

[41] Cabane, *The Charisma Myth*. 158.

[42] Goldman, Daniel, and Richard Boyatzis. "Social Intelligence and the Biology of Leadership." (Boston, MA: *Harvard Business Review*, September 2008).

[43] Lewis, Thomas, M.D., et al., *A General Theory of Love*. (New York: Vintage Books, 2000).

[44] Kellerman, J., and J. Lewis, and J. D. Lang. "Looking and Loving: The Effects of Mutual Gaze on Feelings of Romantic Love." *Journal of Research in Personality*. 23 (1989): 145-61

[45] Hotz, Robert, Lee. "Hear! Hear! Scientist Map What Charisma Sounds Like." New York: *Wall Street Journal*, December 2, 2014.

[46] Cabane, Olivia Fox. *The Charisma Myth:- How Anyone Can Master the Art and Science of Personal Magnetism*. (New York: Penguin Group, 2013), 144.

[47] Di Pellegrino, G., et al (1992). "Understanding Motor Events: A Neurophysiological Study." *Experimental Brain Research*, 91, 176-180.

[48] King James Bible: Proverbs 29:18

[49] Cadbury, Deborah. *Chocolate Wars: The 150-Year Rivalry Between the World's Greatest Chocolate Makers* (New York: Public Affairs)

[50] Brenner, Joel Glenn. *The Emperors of Chocolate: Inside the Secret World of Hershey and Mars* (New York: Random House, 1999).

[51] Dixon. *The Challenger Sale*.

[52] Ibid.

[53] Gilmore. *The Experience Economy*.

About the Author

One of Kordell's clients said, "Watching Kordell present is like watching popcorn pop . . . without the lid."

His 60+ years of "personal research" into the subject of this book is a life's calling. Kordell is the author of seven books, a Certified Speaking Professional (CSP) and member of the National Speakers Association. He is an expert in customer relationships for sales training, customer service, marketing and branding, and leadership. His presentations to corporate, education, government and association audiences are entertaining, humorous, and jam packed with information that helps others get out of the box, and yet inspire others to higher levels of success.

He is a frequent guest faculty member to universities and colleges, and is a contributor to newspapers and magazines, including *U.S. News & World Report, Travel + Leisure International, Retail Leader, American Chamber of Commerce Executives, Speaker Magazine*, and other trade and industry publications.

A former executive with several multi-Billion dollar corporations he has walked the talk as:

- Vice President of 500 agent Call Centers where 250,000 phone calls were processed each month to drive a $2.5 billion dollar business.
- Director of Human Resources for 5,600 employees

- Director of Marketing with a $30+ million dollar budget to promote some little names like IBM, Microsoft, Apple, Hewlett-Packard, Cisco and others.
- Regional Sales Manager

Kordell loves customers. Whether it is training sales people, facilitating strategic planning sessions for leadership teams as a graphic facilitator, conducting customer service workshops, or entertaining as an interactive speaker, his common interest is in moving the customer relationship to the next level.

Most of all he loves his 6 kids and a banquet of grandchildren.

He can be reached at www.KordellNorton.com or kordell@kordellnorton.com